THE
SUFI CHIVALRY

كِتَابُ الفُتُوَّة

لأبي عبد الرحمن محمد بن الحسين بن موسى السلمي

قدس الله سره العزيز

THE WAY OF SUFI CHIVALRY

*When the Light of the heart
is reflected in the beauty of the face,
that beauty is
FUTUWWAH*

Ibn al-Husayn al-Sulami

*An interpretation by
Tosun Bayrak al-Jerrahi*

Inner Traditions International
Rochester, Vermont

Inner Traditions International
One Park Street
Rochester, Vermont 05767
www.InnerTraditions.com

Inner Traditions would like to express appreciation to the Halveti-Jerrahi Order of
America for its help and cooperation i making this book possible. We also thank
Sheikh al-Hajj Tosun Bayrak al-Jerrahi al-Halveti for providing the calligraphy on
the cover of this book.

Library of Congress Cataloging-in-Publication Data

Sulami, Muhammad ibn al-Husayn, d. 1021.
    [Futūwah.   English]
      The way of Sufi chivalry : when the light of the heart is
reflected in the beauty of the face, that beauty is futuwwah / Ibn
al-Husayn al-Sulami : an interpretation by Tosun Bayrak al-Jerrahi.
        p.   cm.
    Translation of: al-Futūwah.
    Reprint. Originally published: New York : Inner Traditions, c1983.
    Includes bibliographical references.
    ISBN 978-0-89281-317-9
    1. Sufism—Early works to 1800.   2. Sutuwwa—Early works to 1800.
I. Bayrak, Toson.   II. Title.
BP189.6.S8813   1991
297' .4—dc20   91-9872
                                            CIP

Printed in the United States of America.

14   13   12

CONTENTS

TRANSLATOR'S NOTE

This is the first English translation of Sulami's *Kitab al-futuwwah*. It is based on the original Arabic text, taken from a manuscript in the library of the Hagia Sophia Museum in Istanbul (vol. 2049, folio 78a-99a). The English translation, although true to the meaning of the original, required some changes in vocabulary and grammatical structure in order to make it easier to read and more comprehensible to the Western reader. For similar reasons, the citation of authorities of transmission has been simplified (see the Isnad following the text).

My thanks are due to my revered master, teacher, and guide along the way to Truth, Sheikh Muzaffer Ozak al-Jerrahi al-Halveti, who taught me, according to my humble capacity, the Futuwwah and everything else I know. May God grant him long life to be a blessing for all seekers of Truth.

I wish to acknowledge my gratefulness to Professor Suleyman Ateş, whose Turkish translation of this book has been of the greatest assistance.

May God be pleased with Zaineb Istrabadi, who reviewed the manuscript; with Zehra Lowenthal, who checked the English and typed the manuscript; with Claudine Fisher and Kendra Crossen, who edited it; with Rabia Harris, who typed, transliterated, and made corrections in the translation, all with careful attention to important details; and with all my dervishes, who inspired me to translate this work in order to help them become what God meant Man to be.

We hope that this book will be beneficial for those who are involved in Islam and Sufism in the West. This humble servant of God prays that these words find their mark. May the readers find wisdom and salvation, and may God grant His approval.

FOREWORD

ON SULAMI AND HIS TIMES

Abu 'Abdul-Rahman Muhammad ibn al-Husayn ibn Muhammad ibn Musa ibn Khalid ibn Salim ibn Rawia al-Sulami was born on April 16 in the year 936 C.E. (A.H. 325) in Nishapur, and met his Lord on November 3, 1021 (A.H. 412) in the same city.

His father, al-Husayn ibn Muhammad ibn Musa, a well-known Sufi teacher, initiated Sulami into Islamic mysticism during the boy's early childhood. Ibn Musa later left his family and retired to Mecca. From that time onward, Sulami lived with and learned from his maternal grandfather, 'Amr Isma'il ibn Nujayd, who was considered one of the greatest theologians of his time. The wealthy grandfather became a father, teacher, and benefactor to Sulami. The depth of the relationship is reflected in the grandson's taking the name Sulami, which was the name of his mother's tribe (Sulaym). Ibn Nujayd kept the young Sulami by his side during lectures and discussion that he held with other great men of the time.

Sulami's traditional education began with the memorizing of the Koran. He then studied with grammarians and literary men, and became a great transmitter of Prophetic traditions and interpreter of the Koran.

He traveled to many cities of Khorasan and Turkestan, to Iraq and to the Hijaz (Arabia). Although he did not record any visits to Syria or Egypt, he seems to have intimately known the countries between Samarkand and Balkh to the east and Cairo and Mecca to the west. Apparently he did not travel in countries west of Egypt or the Maghrib (North Africa and Spain), as he rarely mentions the Sufi saints of these lands.

During his travels, Sulami collected the wisdom of many saints, and later he quoted them in his works, specifically in the *Tabaqat al-sufiyyah* (Classes of Sufis), where he mentions one hundred and five Sufis and their teachings. In Baghdad and Mecca he methodically interviewed many Sufi teachers, and it was in those cities that he gathered most of his knowledge.

In addition to the wisdom gathered from knowledgeable Sufis of his time, Sulami also learned from the writings of his grandfather and from the vast library that he inherited from the older man. Many of the saints mentioned in Sulami's books were themselves authors, although most of their work has not survived the passage of time.

The mystical movement that created Sufism culminated in the ninth and tenth centuries (A.H. third and fourth centuries). By the year 996 (A.H. 386) a Sufi named Talib al-Makki reported that Junayd, who died in 909 (A.H. 297), was the last true representative of Sufism. In his *Risalah* or Essay (1045 C.E.; A.H. 437), al-Qushayri, a student of Sulami's, wrote complaining that Sufism and religion were coming to an end. Such complaints, which continue today, seem by their very existence to contradict themselves, although it is true that Sufism reached its peak at about the time of the martyrdom of Hallaj, who made the famous declaration "I am the Truth" in 922 (A.H. 309). His execution epitomized the violent confrontation between the *shari'ah* (the orthodoxy that dominated Islam) and the *tariqah* (mysticism), but did not end the struggle, although this tragedy helped to bring orthodoxy and mysticism closer together. We can see in the teachings of Sulami, Qushayri, Imam Ghazali, and 'Abdul-Qadir al-Jilani, that it created a fusion of the inner and outer aspects of Islam, producing the union and interdependence of *shari'ah* and *tariqah*. Sulami was a pioneer in his attempt to establish this synthesis, a union not only of orthodoxy and mysticism, but also of the divergent disciplines within Sufism. A new science, *'ilm al-tasawwuf*, the science of Sufism, was created, one that gathered data on the mystical experience of various saints and the schools they represented. These experiences are substantiated by the support of the Koran and the *Sunnah* (practice) of the Prophet (s.a.w.s.).* According to this science, there are three distinct levels of knowledge: first is *'ilm al-yaqin*, knowledge through information; second, *'ayn al-yaqin*, knowledge, through experience; and third and highest, *haqq al-yaqin*, true knowledge through being. A code of conduct for the daily life of the Sufis was established in all its aspects, social, economic, and psychological. The propagator of the knowledge had to live by this code and experience its three levels. The three most important books written on the subject are *Kitab al-luma'* by Nasr al-Tusi al-Sarraj (d. 988 C.E.; A.H. 378), one of Sulami's teachers; *Tabaqat al-sufiyyah* by Sulami (1021 C.E.; A.H. 412); and the *Risalah* of 'Abdul-Karim al-Qushayri (d. 1074 C.E.; A.H. 465). These works became textbooks for posterity.

*The abbreviation "s.a.w.s." stands for *salla Allahu 'alayhi wa sallam*, "May Allah commend and salute him," an honorific phrase that accompanies mention of the Prophet Muhammad.

These texts of Sufi wisdom, collected by Sulami and other saints who were his contemporaries, gained great importance and reputation, and they even began to be used in mosques, where previously only Hadith (the traditions of the Prophet, s.a.w.s.) and the Holy Koran had been taught. The sheikhs taught this science of conscious being not as an abstract philosophy but as a way of life supported by the doctrine of Islamic orthodoxy.

Sulami's *Way of Sufi Chivalry* is such a teaching, synthesizing the unification of orthodox and mystical paths. This code of Sufi morals proposes to lead man to consciousness and perfection. It reveals the true meaning of compassion, love, friendship, generosity, self-denial, hospitality, and the right actions associated with these virtues.

ON FUTUWWAH

Futuwwah is the way of the *fata*. In Arabic, *fata* literally means a handsome, brave youth. After the enlightenment of Islam, following the use of the word in the Holy Koran, *fata* (plural: *fityan*) came to mean the ideal, noble, and perfect man whose hospitality and generosity would extend until he had nothing left for himself; a man who would give all, including his life, for the sake of his friends. According to the Sufis, Futuwwah is a code of honorable conduct that follows the example of the prophets, saints, sages, and the intimate friends and lovers of Allah.

The traditional example of generosity is the prophet Abraham, peace be upon him, who readily accepted the command to sacrifice his son for Allah's sake. He is also a model of hospitality who shared his meals with guests all his life and never ate alone. The prophet Joseph, peace be upon him, is an example of mercy, for he pardoned his brothers, who tried to kill him, and a model of honor, for he resisted the advances of a married woman, Zulaykha, who was feminine beauty personified. The principles of character of the four divinely guided caliphs, the successors of the Prophet Muhammad, peace and blessings be upon him, also served as guides to Futuwwah; the loyalty of Abu Bakr, the justice of 'Umar, the reserve and modesty of 'Uthman, and the bravery of 'Ali, may Allah be pleased with them all.

The all-encompassing symbol of the way of Futuwwah is the divinely guided life and character of the final prophet, Muhammad Mustafa, may Allah's peace and blessings be upon him, whose perfection is the goal of Sufism. The Sufi aims to abandon all improper behavior and to acquire and exercise, always and under all circumstances, the best behavior proper to human beings; for God created man "for Himself" as His "supreme creation," "in the fairest form." As He declares in His Holy Koran, "We have indeed honored the children of Adam."

The following stories take place in the time of the caliphate of 'Umar ibn al-Khattab (r.a.a.),* the second of the divinely guided caliphs who governed after the Prophet (s.a.w.s.), who himself married 'Umar's daughter. Known as al-'Adil, the Just, 'Umar was a true inspiration of virtue, a knight and warrior during whose rule Syria, Iraq, Iran, and Egypt were added to the Islamic dominions. He was humble and wore patched clothes. He never sat on a throne, and he

---

*The abbreviation "r.a.a." stands for radiya Allahu 'anhu, "May Allah be well pleased with him," the prayer attached to the names of the companions of the Prophet (s.a.w.s.).

ate at the same table with his servants. He was true to his word, generous, loyal, and a symbol of strength who inspired fear in the hearts of the enemies of Truth.

Hazrat 'Umar reported:
One day the Messenger of Allah asked us for donations. The desire came to me to surpass Abu Bakr, who had always been ahead of me in every good deed. I brought a fortune representing half of all I possessed and came to the presence of the Prophet (s.a.w.s.), and told our Master that my donation was half of all that I had, and the other half I had left for the support of my family. Abu Bakr came in with a large sack of gold and placed it at the feet of our Master. Our Master asked him what percentage of his wealth his donation represented. He answered, "All of it." Then the Messenger of Allah, looking at me, asked Abu Bakr, "Why haven't you kept anything for your children?" Abu Bakr answered, "My children are in the care of Allah and His Messenger."

After that incident Abu Bakr was not visible for a few days, and did not appear at the mosque of the Prophet (s.a.w.s). Feeling a void in the absence of Abu Bakr, the Prophet asked his whereabouts. The companions answered that Abu Bakr had distributed all his possessions and that he had nothing to wear except a piece of cloth, which he shared with his wife, each of them using it alternately to wrap themselves at the time of prayer. At that time the Prophet (s.a.w.s.) asked Bilal al-Habashi to go to the house of the Prophet's daughter, Fatimah, and ask her if she had an extra piece of cloth that could be brought to Abu Bakr so that he could clothe himself and come to the mosque. All that the noble Fatimah had was one extra piece of cloth made of goat hair. When Abu Bakr wrapped it around his waist, it was too short. So he sewed some date palm leaves to it so that he could cover himself decently, and took the road to the mosque.

Before he arrived, Gabriel appeared to our Master in the same unseemly outfit that Abu Bakr was wearing. When the Prophet (s.a.w.s.) said to Gabriel that he had never seen him in such strange clothes, Gabriel replied that today all the angels in heaven were so dressed to honor Hazrat Abu Bakr, the loyal, generous, and faithful. Allah Most High was sending blessings and salutations to Abu Bakr. Gabriel said: "Tell him his Lord is pleased with Him if he is pleased with his Lord." When Abu Bakr came into the presence of our Master and heard the good news from the lips of the beloved Prophet (s.a.w.s.), he got up, thanked Allah, said, "Indeed I am pleased with my Lord!" and in his joy whirled around three times.

(It is in this way that the whirling dervishes whirl today.)

One day, during the caliphate of Hazrat 'Umar, while he was sitting with his companions, three noble and beautiful young men entered his presence. Two of them said, "We two are brothers. While our father was working in his field, he was killed by this young man, whom we have brought to you for justice. Punish him according to God's Book." The caliph turned to the third young man and asked him to speak.

"Although there were no witnesses, Allah, the Ever-

Present, knows they are telling the truth," said the accused. "I regret very much that their father found death at my hands. I am a villager. I arrived in Medina this morning to visit the tomb of our Prophet, may Allah commend and salute him. At the outskirts of the city I got off my horse to take ablution. My horse started eating from the branch of a date tree that was hanging over a wall. As soon as I noticed this, I pulled my horse away from the branch. At that moment an angry old man approached with a big stone in his hand. He threw the stone at my horse's head, killing it instantly. Since I loved my horse very much, I lost control of myself. I picked up the stone and threw it back at the man. He fell dead. If I had wanted to escape, I could have done so, but to where? If I do not meet my punishment here, I shall meet an eternal punishment in the hereafter. I had not intended to kill this man, but he died by my hand. Now the judgment is yours."

The caliph said, "You have committed murder. According to Islamic law, you must receive treatment equal to that which you have dispensed."

Although this was a pronouncement of death, the young man kept his composure and calmly said, "So be it. However, a fortune has been left in my care to be given to an orphan when he comes of age. I buried this fortune for safekeeping. Nobody knows where it is but me. I must dig it up and leave it in somebody else's care; otherwise the orphan will be denied his right. Give me three days to go to my village and attend to this duty."

'Umar replied, "Your request cannot be accorded unless somebody takes your place and vouches for your life."

"O Ruler of the Faithful," said the young man, "I could have escaped before if I had wished. My heart is filled with the fear of God; be certain I will be back."

10

The caliph refused on the basis of the Law. The young man looked at the noble companions of the Prophet (s.a.w.s.) who were gathered around the caliph. Choosing at random, he pointed to Abu Dharr al-Ghifari and said, "This man will be the one to vouch for me." Abu Dharr was one of the most beloved and respected companions of the Prophet (s.a.w.s.). Without hesitation he agreed to replace the young man.

The accused was released. On the third day, the two young accusers came back to the caliph's court. Abu Dharr was there, but not the accused. The accusers said, "O Abu Dharr, you vouched for someone you did not know. Even if he does not return, we will not leave without receiving the price of our father's blood."

The caliph said, "Indeed, if the young man does not return, we will have to apply his punishment to Abu Dharr." Hearing this, everyone present began to weep, for Abu Dharr, a man of perfect virtue and splendid character, was the light and inspiration for all of Medina.

When the third day had come to an end, the excitement, sorrow, and amazement of the people reached their peak. Suddenly the young man appeared. He had been running and was tired, dusty, and hot. "I am sorry to have worried you," he said breathlessly. "Pardon me for arriving at the last minute. There was much work to be done, the desert is hot, and the trip was long. I am now ready; execute my punishment."

Then he turned to the crowd and said, "The man of faith is loyal to his word. The one who fails to keep his word is a hypocrite. Who can escape death, which comes sooner or later anyway? Did you think I was going to disappear and make people say, 'The Muslims do not keep their word anymore'?"

11

The crowd then turned to Abu Dharr and asked whether he had known of the young man's fine character. He answered, "Not at all, but I did not feel that I could refuse him when he singled me out, as it would not have been in keeping with the laws of generosity. Should I be the one to make people say that there is no more kindness left in Islam?"

The hearts of the accusers trembled and they dropped their claim, saying, "Should *we* be the ones to make people say that there is no more compassion left in Islam?"

Ibn 'Abbas, companion of the Prophet (s.a.w.s.) and his cousin, who was known as the wisest man of his time, tells of a battle against the nonbelievers, whose army numbered ten times that of the Muslims.

> The battle raged a whole day. Both sides had casualties in proportion to their numbers. When the fighting ceased near sunset, I took a waterskin and went to the battlefield, which was full of dead and wounded men. I heard many among the Muslims groaning and asking for water. I approached one dying soldier whose lips were parched. As I was about to make him drink, we heard another close by begging for water. The wounded hero asked me to give the water to the other soldier first. When I went to the second man, we heard a nearby enemy soldier begging for water. The Muslim asked me to first give the water to him. When I had served water to the wounded enemy, I returned to the Muslim warrior, but he had already drunk the wine of martyrdom. I went back to the first soldier, but he too had met his Lord.

Such is the scope of generosity and compassion in Futuwwah.

Such prominent virtues of Islam as are illustrated in this story are based on the behavior of the Prophet Muhammad (s.a.w.s.), the members of his family, and the four caliphs who inherited his perfect character. This is the foundation of the philosophy of Futuwwah. Futuwwah is a state of mind. It means placing other people above oneself. It is being generous and altruistic. It is self-denial, immunity to disappointment, indulgence toward other people's shortcomings. It is a fearless struggle against tyranny, and above all, it is love. Love is the essence of Futuwwah; love of God, love of His creation, love of Love.

Hazrat 'Ali (r.a.a.), the last of the divinely guided caliphs, the Lion of Allah, the symbol of knowledge, generosity, and loyalty, the father of the grandchildren of the Prophet (s.a.w.s.), was also known as the invincible warrior of his time. In one battle he had overpowered an enemy warrior and had his dagger at the man's throat when the nonbeliever spat in his face. Immediately Hazrat 'Ali got up, sheathed his dagger, and told the man, "Taking your life is unlawful to me. Go away!" The man, who had saved his life by spitting in the face of the revered Lion of Allah, was amazed. "O 'Ali," he asked, "I was helpless, you were about to kill me, I insulted you and you released me. Why?" "When you spat in my face," Hazrat 'Ali answered, "it aroused the anger of my ego. Had I killed you then it would not have been for the sake of Allah, but for the sake of my ego. I would have been a murderer. You are free to go." The enemy warrior, moved by the integrity displayed in Hazrat 'Ali, converted to Islam on the spot.

In another of his battles against the unfaithful, Hazrat 'Ali encountered a handsome young warrior who moved to attack

13

him. His heart filled with pity and compassion for the misguided youth. He cried out, "O young man, do you not know who I am? I am 'Ali the invincible. No one can escape from my sword. Go, and save yourself!" The young man continued toward him, sword in hand. "Why do you wish to attack me?" 'Ali said. "Why do you wish to die?"

The young man answered, "I love a girl who vowed she would be mine if I killed you."

"But what if *you* die?" 'Ali asked.

"What is better than dying for the one I love?" he replied. "At worst, would I not be relieved of the agonies of love?"

Hearing this response, 'Ali dropped his sword, took off his helmet, and stretched his neck like a sacrificial lamb.

Confronted by such an action, the love in the young man's heart was transformed into love for 'Ali and the One Whom 'Ali loved.

Already during Sulami's lifetime, the principles of brotherhood, loyalty, love, and honor derived from the code of Sufi chivalry had begun to produce a distinct class of people with special social responsibilities. Later, during the reign of Caliph al-Nasir al-Din Allah (1180-1125 C.E.; A.H. 575-622), the rank of Futuwwah was accorded to worthy princes and dignitaries. Such men were ceremonially dressed in special vestments and made to drink from the cup of knighthood. The images of the cup and the vestment appeared on their coats of arms. The oaths they swore were unconditionally respected.

In Syria, the members of this brotherhood were responsible for the rebellion against the heretical Rafidites. In Asia Minor, the brotherhood developed into fraternal communities whose members lived in convents under the guidance of a sheikh, and often all worked at the same trade. The clothing that distinguished them consisted of a cloak, a white woolen cap, and shoes particular to them, and each wore a knife in his belt. It is reported that they were hospitable to travelers and ruthless toward tyrannical rulers. Futuwwah later became one of the essential elements in the Islamic guilds.

The rules of conduct and virtues presented in *The Way of Sufi Chivalry* illuminate the way to the total assimilation of Sufism by experiencing and living it. This code of honor leads to a state of total consciousness of Truth, not by hearing it or by seeing it, but by *being* it.

This is the book of *adab*, perfect behavior, modeled after the Prophet Muhammad (s.a.w.s.). The Sufis see *adab* as a continuous act of devotion, for it is a method of constant remembrance of God, an alarm clock ever ringing, reminding one that the reason for one's existence is to know, to find, and to be with God. As God Himself said to His Prophet, "I was a hidden treasure. I loved to be known, so I created Man."

INTRODUCTION

The Arabic word *futuwwah* is the keystone of this book, which was perhaps the first ever devoted to this subject. Many different definitions of the word are given by the spiritual masters cited by Sulami.[1] This should not surprise us, for their aim was not to formulate a universal doctrine, but rather to inform the heart, taking into account the possibilities and shortcomings of their disciples. Moreover, the comments of these master bear the imprint of their individual natures and degrees of spiritual attainment. Yet despite the multiplicity of viewpoints expressed in their words and deeds, all focus on one central notion: that of "heroic generosity."

Sulami has provided us with extraordinary examples of this admirable virtue. But from a gnostic, an *'arif billah,* should we not expect more than just a lesson in ethical behavior, however noble and chivalrous? Haven't these men of God more to tell us? Indeed they do, if we are able to perceive the subtle meaning of their words. Nevertheless, it was the task of later Masters, when cyclical conditions so demanded, to elucidate the hidden meaning of these blunt sayings, and even to give Futuwwah an institutionalized form. As a result, the many contrasts in the interpretations of the term became more pronounced—or at least they appeared so on the surface. As we shall see, this seeming variance masks a deep, innate coherence, for in fact, all that pertains to Futuwwah in the Islamic tradition is connected with supreme Knowledge.

At the time that Caliph al-Nasir al-Din Allah ascended to the throne in 1180, Islam was weakened by internal strife, harassed on all its borders, and on the brink of formidable disturbances. Genghis Khan was only thirteen years old then, but as early as 1206 he would be recognized as the "universal monarch" of the Mongols. Within a few decades, a gradual but irreversible tidal wave would submerge the 'Abbasid empire, and in 1258, thiry-three years after al-Nasir's death, the Mongols would raze Baghdad, its capital. The Mongolian threat was still remote in 1180, but another danger, stemming from the West, had already been brewing for a century. The first Crusades had begun in 1095, and Jerusalem had fallen to the Christians by 1099. Saladin would reconquer this third-holiest city of Islam in 1187, but other crusades would follow until the end of the thirteenth century. As the storm was gathering on its borders, the caliphate was dying. The Seljuk Turks, contesting the caliphs' power, had undermined the strength of the institution. Independent dynasties were created in Asia Minor, Syria, and Iran. In Egypt, the Fatimid anticaliphate had disappeared, but the Ayyubids remained an autonomous power.

This disintegration of the *ummah* (community of the faithful) not only led to the ruin of the caliph's worldly power, but also jeopardized the *amanah,* the "sacred trust" of which Islam is the guardian. Al-Nasir, faced with this peril during his reign, undertook the task of restoring the conditions appropriate to the safekeeping of the *amanah.* Although his failures were numerous and his victories precarious in the political and military domains, his efforts nevertheless were immense, and he deserves more than mere homage to his courage—that is, if one is not satisfied with a

17

profane interpretation of history, but wishes instead to decipher the interplay of the spiritual forces that ultimately determine the true course of events.

During the two centuries preceding the fall of Baghdad, a providential readjustment took place, of which al-Nasir's efforts are but a part.[2] The significance of this gradual transformation probably eluded most of the people of that time. In any case, it would allow for the transmission of the *amanah,* despite the dislocation of traditional structures, which culminated in 1258 with the extinction of the 'Abbasid dynasty.

It was the era of al-Ghazali (d. 1111), the most famous reconciler of orthodox and mystical Islam, and of Ibn 'Arabi (d. 1240), *al-shaykh al-akbar,* the spiritual master par excellence. With them appeared the great doctrinal syntheses that would guarantee the perpetuity of spiritual teachings, which more ancient and allusive modes would not have sufficed to preserve. It was also during this era that Sufism coalesced, so to speak, from a fluid state to a solid one, and became organized into orders, ensuring its survival and its ability to act as an anchor in a confused world where entropy had brutally accelerated.

Finally, it was also the time in which Futuwwah was, through al-Nasir's initiative, officially institutionalized. In a famous article published in 1849, the Orientalist Hammer-Purgstall interpreted this event as the birth of a chivalric order among the Arabs.[3] This conclusion, which was based on a cursory examination of very few sources, may be excessive and may deserve some of the scholarly criticism it received later on; nevertheless, the Christian and Islamic institutions present striking similarities. For example, in the West, the

Templars asked a monk, Saint Bernard, to codify the rule of their order; in Baghdad, when al-Nasir institutionalized Futuwwah, which also had a military vocation, he called upon a great Sufi, Shihab al-Din al-Suhrawardi (d. 1234), the founder of the order (tariqah) that bears his name, to give it its code and ritual.

The Nasirian Futuwwah expressed the caliph's grand design: for him, the reconquest of the lost territories, the defense of the threatened borders, and the reestablishment of the caliphal authority lost to unruly vassals were meaningless if not linked with a spiritual rectification to which the military caste had to be associated. Whence the birth, under al-Nasir's patronage, of an initiatic, organized order, which borrowed Sufi doctrines and methods and linked its initiatic chain (silsilah) to the Sufi masters, but possessed its own distinct character, such as the ritualized practice of hunting and of martial arts. Multiple sources document the hierarchy of ranks; the rituals that gave access to each rank (in which an important role was given to a symbolic beverage, the cup of salted water, as well as to the investiture of the novice with a belt comparable in function to the khirqah, the cloak or robe of the Sufis); the code of ethics emphasizing honor, generosity, and bravery; and the esoteric meaning of this "aristocratic" or "courtly" Futuwwah.[4] Al-Nasir's death, the succession of mediocre rulers, and, finally, the fall of the 'Abbasid caliphate, obliterated any hope of restoring a traditional Islamic order, centered on what Henri Corbin calls "spiritual chivalry." The Nasirian Futuwwah and some of its branches continued to survive for a while in Anatolia, for example, or in Egypt, where the Mamluk sultan welcomed a member of the 'Abbasid family who had been spared in the

19

Mongol slaughter, and conferred upon him a nominal caliphate. He, in turn, invested the sultan with the "cloak of Futuwwah," a ceremony that continued among their successors for more than a century. But though the form persisted, the spirit had withdrawn and the initial radiance had dulled.

At the same time, however, another Futuwwah asserted itself, a popular one, this time linked to artisanship, and it has continued to our times, under different names: *fata*, in Arabic, *akhi*, in Turkish, and *javanmard* in Persian, for example, all signify an adherent of Futuwwah. The initiatic rites of this popular Futuwwah, which include the cup of salted water and the investiture of the belt, present many similarities to the "aristocratic" Futuwwah, but they also use symbolic objects, gestures, and technical terms related to the trades.[5] This popular Futuwwah is both distinct from Sufism and symbiotically related to it. Like Sufism, it possesses an essentially spiritual finality to which are subordinated, at least in principle, more visible activities, be they economic, social, or political. Both Sufism and Futuwwah are rooted in a distant past, and both became structured at about the same time.

The word *futuwwah* is not found in the Arabic language at the beginning of Islam. However, it is derived from a very ancient word, *fata*, whose basic meaning is "young man" (*shabb*): one who, though having reached adulthood, has not yet arrived at maturity (traditionally achieved at age forty), which is the time of plenitude, but also the beginning of decline. This meaning of *fata* includes a heroic connotation that has become inseparable from the term *futuwwah*. The ideal *fata*, who is exemplified by 'Ali, cousin and son-in-law of the Prophet, is characterized by selflessness, courage, generosity, and honor.

Proceeding from the external to the internal, I have chosen to consider first the institutional aspect of Futuwwah. Although the characteristics noted so far help us to understand what kinds of behavior Futuwwah manifests, they have not yet shed direct light on its essence. Before continuing, let us first recall that the concepts we are discussing are not the product of individual initiative or of mere speculation, which, even though expressed in an Islamic vocabulary, would ultimately be exogenous aggregates grafted onto original Islam. On the contrary, they may be traced to the Koranic revelation itself. Thus, the search for scriptural support for these doctrines, esoteric practices, or technical terms is not just an intellectual game or a clever tactic designed to prevent attacks by the ulema, but a sure way to reach an understanding of their essential truth *(haqiqah)*.

The term *fata* appears often in the Koran. The meditation of the people of Futuwwah *(ahl al-futuwwah)* has always been most particularly centered on the occurrence of this word in verse 60 of chapter 21 *(Surah al-Anbiya', The Prophets)*, where it is applied to Abraham, who has just destroyed the idols worshipped by his people and so is about to be cast into the furnace by the infidels.[6] In a chapter devoted to Futuwwah in his celebrated *Risalah,* Qushayri, a direct disciple of Sulami's, reports a definition of *fata* inspired by that Koranic episode: "The *fata* is he who breaks the idol."[7] Qushayri immediately adds a pithy commentary that leads us to the threshold of the mystery of Futuwwah: "And the idol of each man is his ego." Here, then, is the metaphysical truth hidden in the sayings of the Masters as related by Sulami and others—sayings that merely describe the means of access to this truth or the effects of it on those who embody it. Therefore, the true Futuwwah is nothing more, but nothing less, than man's effective realization of his radical ontological indigence and, with the destruction of the illusory ego, the unveiling of that which is and always will be the Unique Reality.

Along the path that leads to this end, the *fata* must first learn not to love his ego, and that is why, in the course of his novitiate, the sheikh teaches him to love others before himself, and God above all.[8] But once the goal has been attained, he discovers that the secret of his apprenticeship is that he has no ego, and what he loved was but a dream. The idol has reverted to nothingness; both "self" and "others" cease to exist. For him, the trials of spiritual combat have now become, like the furnace to Abraham (Koran 21:69), "refreshment and peace" *(bardan wa salaman)*.

The advent of this irrevocable certitude is marked by an initiatic event, often designated as the "opening" or "conquest" *(fath)*.[9] This event is indescribable, and its nature can only be suggested by recourse to symbol. It is therefore significant that some of the symbolic expressions of this denouement lead us again to the *fata*. However, in this last act of the quest, in which until now the *fata* figured as the hero, he will be metamorphosed (in the strictest meaning of the word) before our very eyes. Having arrived at this ultimate stage, the *fata* in effect is no longer he who seeks, but he who is found.

At the beginning of *al-Futuhat al-Makkiyyah*, the major work of the man who, for many Muslims, is the "Seal of Muhammadan Sanctity," Ibn 'Arabi describes a meeting in Mecca, before the Kaaba, with an enigmatic personage whom he calls "the young man" *(al-fata)*.[10] This nameless "young man" is described as "he who speaks and is silent" *(al-mutakallim al-samit)*, "who is neither dead nor alive" *(laysa bi-*

hayyin wa la ma'it). He is at the same time "simple and composed" *(al-murakkab al-basit);* he is "contained by all things and contains all things" *(al-muhat al-muhit).* He transcends "the where and the when" that is, space and time. He is "the knowledge, the known, and the knowing" *(al-'ilm wa l-ma'lum wa l-'alim)* or "the contemplating and the contemplated" *(al-shahid wa l-mashhud).* It is from the "nature" of this "young man" that Ibn 'Arabi says he has drawn "all that is written in this book."

Who is this *fata* whom Ibn 'Arabi describes sometimes as a spirit *(ruh)* or an angel *(malak)* and sometimes as a human being *(insiyyun)*—all the while suggesting, by the attributes assigned to him, that he is of a divine nature and is in fact no less than a theophany? Some of Ibn 'Arabi's allusive sentences allow us to decipher this paradox without hesitation: for example, when, addressing the *fata,* he affirms seeing in him "the equal and the peer" and when he declares at the end of a dialogue with this mysterious interlocutor, "who only speaks in symbols" *(la yukallimu ahadan illa ramzan):* "He revealed to me all my names, and I knew who I was and who I was not." We understand that this *fata,* this luminous double, confronts him, in a vision whose beauty transfigures him, with the essence of his own reality; thus he has become that which he has been for all eternity.

We again meet this *fata* in another text by Ibn 'Arabi, *Kitab al-isra,* (The Book of Nocturnal Voyage).[11] This encounter happens "at the source of Arin." The very name gives us a key to the interpretation of what will follow. In traditional Islamic geography, Arin designates an island, or a mythical city, equidistant from north and south and from east and west. It is obviously a symbolic denomination of the supreme spiritual center, or, microcosmically speaking, of what is often represented in sacred anthropology as the "heart." This is also the very significance of the place where the preceding story was taking place. Mecca, "mother of cities" (Koran 6:92), is, in effect, according to a tradition going back to Ibn 'Abbas, "the navel of the earth" (surrat al-ard), and the Kaaba, the Black Stone, which is "in the world" without being "of the world," for it is of celestial origin, is its "pivot."[12] There can be no doubt that the fata who, at the source of Arin, teaches the voyager, is identical to the one whose appearance opens the 560th chapter of the Futuhat, for we hear him address his companion in these terms: "You are the cloud that veils your own sun. Know the essential reality of your being."[13] It is then clear that the fata does not merely answer: he is the answer.[14] Thus, its ultimate secret laid bare, the cycle of Futuwwah comes to an end.

Michel Chodkiewicz

NOTES

1. On Sulami and his work, see Brockelmann, Geschichte der arabischen Litteratur, I, 218, and p. 361, and Sezgin, Geschichte des arabischen Schrifftums, I, 671 ff. The first critical edition of Kitab al-futuwwah is Franz Taeschner's in Studia orientalia Joanni Pedersen...dicta (Copenhagen, 1953), pp. 340-351.

2. For a deeper study of al-Nasir, see Angelika Hartmann, al-Nasir li-Din Allah (Berlin and New York, 1975).

3. J. von Hammer-Purgstall, "Sur la chevalerie des arabes," Journal Asiatique (Paris, 1849).

4. The terms *aristocratic* and *courtly* are usually used by historians to distinguish Nasirian Futuwwah from the "popular" variety. On the different forms of Futuwwah and their evolution, chiefly considered from a social-historical point of view, see, in the *Encyclopedia of Islam* (new ed., II, 961 ff.), the articles by Claude Cahen (for the pre-Mongol period) and Franz Taeschner (for the post-Mongol period). These articles include a vast bibliography, to which must be added an essential work, the *Rasa'il-i javanmardan* (Teheran and Paris, 1973), a collection in Persian of seven *futuwwat-nameh* (treatises on Futuwwah) edited by Morteza Sarraf. This anthology includes two works by Suhrawardi which formulate the statutes of the Nasirian Futuwwah and highlight its esoteric character. A long analytical introduction, written in French by Henri Corbin, has been separately published under the title *Traité des compagnons-chevaliers*. It constitutes a fundamental clarification, despite the author's well-known inclination toward a Shi'ite interpretation.

5. In the case of textile printers, we find a characteristic example of the ritual use and esoteric interpretation of the gestures of the trade in the last of the seven treatises published by Morteza Sarraf (p. 83 ff.). I would like to emphasize in passing an obvious parallelism between Christian and Islamic esoterism. In both we witness the appearance of initiatic organizations (exemplified in Christendom by Masonry and "Compagnnonage") which constitute providential adaptations to specific milieu of the traditional methods toward realization. In the East, as in the West, this adaptation occurred under the control of spiritual authorities, such as Saint Bernard in the case of the Templars, and Suhrawardi, among others, in the case of Futuwwah. For reasons evidently

linked to cyclical conditions, these artisans' initiations outlived those of the knights, and received a part of their spiritual heritage.

6. *Fata* in its plural form *(fityan)* is also applied to the Companions of the Cavern *(ahl al-kahf,* Koran 18:10,13), and in its singular form it designates Moses' companion (Koran 18:60, 62).

7. Qushayri, *Risalah* (Cairo, 1957), pp. 103-105.

8. "The others" in this case embraces the totality of creatures, not only humankind. Ibn 'Arabi, in his *Futuhat* (I, 244; II, 233; cf. anecdote II, 235), emphasizes that the generosity of the *fata* must extend to the mineral, vegetal, and animal kingdoms.

9. The word *fath* is frequently used to designate by analogy a series of initiatic events that represent successive stages in the spiritual journey *(suluk)* and that therefore correspond to the lifting of different "veils" separating man from the essential Reality. I allude here to the ultimate *fath.* Qashani (a master of Ibn 'Arabi's school who died in 1330) wrote a doctrinal exposition on the major distinctions between the different levels of *fath,* based on the various scriptural uses of the word, in his commentary on Surah al-Fath *(Tafsir,* published under the name of Ibn 'Arabi [Beirut, 1968], II, 505-506).

10. See *al-Futuhat al-Makkiyyah* (Cairo, A.H. 1329), chap. 1 (I, 47-57). A detailed and penetrating analysis of this inaugural account (about which, however, I have certain reservations) has been given by Henri Corbin in *L'Imagination créatrice dans le Soufisme d'Ibn 'Arabi* (Paris, 1958), p. 207 ff. The author translates *fata* as *jouvenceau mystique,* "mystical youth." It is worth remarking that Ibn 'Arabi has devoted three chapters to

Futuwwah in his *Futuhat* (chap. 42, I, 241-244, and chaps. 146-147, II, 231-234).

11. Hyderabad, 1948. *Kitab al-isra,* written in Fez in A.H. 594, is in fact anterior to the *Futuhat,* which Ibn 'Arabi began to write in Mecca in A.H. 599. The theme of the nocturnal voyage and of the ascension *(mi'raj),* prototyped by the *mi'raj* of the Prophet, as described in several Hadith, is taken up again in two important chapters of the *Futuhat.* In chap. 167, Ibn 'Arabi allegorically describes the conditions and modes of this journey; in chap. 367, he relates the successive stages of his own ascension.

12. Muhammad al-Makhzumi, *al-Jami al-latif fi fadl Makka* (Cairo, A.H. 1357), p. 18; on *Arin,* see the entry *Istiwa* in *Encyclopedia of Islam.* In his *Istilahat,* Ibn 'Arabi defines *Arin* as "the point of equilibrium of all things."

13. *Kitab al-isra,* p. 4.

14. This encounter with the celestial *fata,* which reveals to certain beings their permanent reality *in divinis,* after they have "broken the idol," can be understood as an anticipation of the paradisiac status of the Elect. We should stress here the significant coherence between initiatic and eschatological symbolism. According to certain traditions (e.g., Baghawi, *Masabih al-Sunnah,* II, 152), the inhabitants of Paradise will all be "beardless young men." They will have "Adam's height and Jesus' age," that is, thirty-three. (The reference to Adam and Jesus, the "second Adam," who, for Ibn 'Arabi, is the Seal of Universal Sanctity, would need a fuller commentary than can be given here.) It is moreover important to note that the authentically Islamic and Muhammadan character of the vision of the essential Reality through the traits of the *fata* is corroborated by a tradition that Ibn 'Arabi cites at the end of

27

chap. 3 of the *Futuhat* (I, 97). In this Hadith, the Prophet states: "I have seen my Lord in the form of a beardless youth." According to Ibn 'Arabi, the "Lord" of every "servant" (that is, of every creature) is nothing other than the Divine Name from which the "servant" draws everything that sustains his being.

ISNAD
THE CHAIN OF AUTHORITIES

In the original Arabic text of *Kitab al-futuwwah,* each paragraph dealing with the codes of behavior in the path of Futuwwah is substantiated either by a Hadith or by the authority of a Sufi saint. Sulami relates these statements through a long chain of authorities of transmission *(isnad),* giving the name of each authority, from the original speaker up to himself. For the sake of easier reading, the translation names only the originator of each statement and the person who told it directly to Sulami. As a sample, the complete chain of authority is given for the first two Hadith mentioned in the text. Thereafter, the statements are numbered to correspond with the numbered chains of authority in the *isnad* section at the end of the book.

Isnad is extremely important in all Islamic religious texts, for a statement has no value unless it is backed up by a witness who heard it, and is guaranteed by a series of authorities who transmitted the words verbatim to each other at times and places that can be historically verified. In the first part of his book, Sulami uses the traditional expression *"akhbarana...ijazatan..."* ("so-and-so informed us on the authority of so-and-so"), with the names of seven or eight transmitters. Toward the end of the book, the *isnad* is reduced to one or two transmitters, and Sulami uses the phrase *"ma qala wa qala"* ("he said that so-and-so said") or sometimes *"wa sami'tu"* ("I heard so-and-so say"). But even in the case of his own personal transmissions, Sulami is careful to cite other witnesses who heard the same statement. At least seventy-seven of the names Sulami mentions are those of sheikhs who lived during his time, and there is good reason to believe that he talked to and worked with them.

THE WAY
OF SUFI CHIVALRY

PART ONE

In the Name of Allah, the Compassionate and the Merciful, on Whom we depend.

All praise is due to Allah Who has opened the path of Futuwwah, which leads to the most beautiful form of the fulfillment of our duties to Him, and Who has cleared and cleansed that path from all errors and all evil and raised its level to the highest. The prophets whom He has sent and the chosen servants who are close to Him are on this path. All for whom the path to Truth has been opened and whose names are written as pure in the Book of Righteousness learned to follow this path and attained the noble levels of those who embody Futuwwah.

The first to follow the call of Futuwwah, to honor munificence and good conduct, was Adam—whose name is fixed in the Will of Allah, whose being lives in the House of Majesty, who is supported by the Holy Light and Purity, and who has been crowned by the Crown of Munificence and entered into the Realm of Salvation. When his son Cain renounced Futuwwah, his other son, Abel, took it up. The prophet Seth gave Futuwwah its due and protected it from all and everything that was improper. The prophet Enoch was brought to high stations by it and was saved from the traps of the Devil. Noah suffered for his devotion to Futuwwah, and thus became illuminated by it. 'Ad was named after Futuwwah, which protected him from pride. Hud showed the beauty of loyalty to his people with Futuwwah, and Salih saved himself from evil with its help. Abraham, the friend of Allah, who was a true *fata,* broke the statues and idols. Through Futuwwah, Ishmael was ready to be sacrificed to his Lord Most High, and Lot reached the high heaven from which there is no descent. With Futuwwah, Isaac prays until the Day of Reckoning. Jacob held fast to the ideals of Futuwwah. In Futuwwah Job found comfort in his sickness. With Futuwwah Joseph trod the most beautiful of paths and succeeded at each step. Dhul-Kifl, abiding with the high ranks of Futuwwah, did his good deeds. Shu'ayb, taking the laurels in the race, won the first place—with Futuwwah he was kept from all doubt and error. Moses was honored by being invested with the robe of Futuwwah. Aaron abode with it and spoke well. The Companions of the Cave and the Inscription were honored by it and were saved and entered into the realm of God's gifts. David's heart was revived with it and because of it he found it sweet to bow and prostrate. Solomon received Futuwwah from David; both men and jinns came to be under his command on its account. Jonah saw Reality in the rules of Futuwwah, and he followed them. Zachariah entered the realm of peace and joy with it. John, with his loyalty to it, in difficult moments was saved from the pangs of suffering. Jesus shone with the purest of light through it, and came to be called the Spirit and the Messiah through it. Entire victory was given to Muhammad, peace and blessings be upon him, and the brothers Abu Bakr and 'Umar and his uncle's son 'Ali became the guardians of it.

O Allah, enable us to act upon this discourse. Accord us the grace of this knowledge. Let us be among those who see the Truth, and lead us on this the best of paths.

Whoever hopes to meet his Lord should do good deeds and worship none but his Lord. (Koran 18:110)

All praise is due to Allah, Whose gifts are eternal, and all power belongs to Allah Most High,

Who begets no son, and has no partner in His dominion; nor needs He any to protect Him from humiliation—yea, magnify Him for His greatness and glory! (Koran 17:111)

All thanks are due to Allah, Who showed the signs of His generosity in His chosen servants, driving them to obedience and saving them from revolt; and informed us that their state is the state of His Friend (s.a.w.s.).

In the Holy Koran He says:

They said: We heard a noble youth [*fata*] called Ibrahim speak of them. (Koran 21:60)

He gave the title *fata* to the one He loves because the one who bears the sign of Futuwwah and is called by its name gives all the love that he had for himself, for his family, for his property and children, to Allah. He empties his being of everything and leaves it to the Owner of All Things. He leaves the whole universe and all that there is in it. That is when Allah calls His chosen friends:

Surely they were noble youths [*fityan*] who believed in their Lord, and We advanced them in guidance. (Koran 18:13)

They were given abundant guidance and climbed to His proximity because they believed in their Lord only for their Lord's sake, and said:

Our Lord is the Lord of Heaven and Earth. Never shall we call upon any god other than Him. (Koran 18:14)

Allah dressed them with His own clothes, and He took them in His high protection and turned them in the direction of His beauties and said:

And We turned them about to the right and to the left. (Koran 18:18)

All who enter the path of Futuwwah are under Allah's direction and protection.

[O my son], may Allah accord you His pleasure. You asked about Futuwwah. Know that Futuwwah means following the ordinances of perfect devotion, leaving all evil, and attaining in action and in thought the best of visible and hidden good conduct. Every condition and every moment demand from you one aspect of Futuwwah. There is no state or time without that demand. There is a Futuwwah fit for your behavior toward God, another toward the Prophet, and others toward his companions; yet others toward the pure ones of the past, your sheikh, your brotherhood, and the two angels on your shoulders who keep the accounting of your deeds.

I shall here describe some of these and support them by the *Sunnah* of the Prophet (s.a.w.s.) and the declarations, actions, conduct, and virtues of our Elders. In this and in all I do, I beseech the aid of Allah, Who suffices me, and Who is the best of guardians.

Bring joy into the lives of your friends and meet their needs. In a Hadith that comes to us through 'Abdul-Rahman ibn Muhammad ibn Mahmud—Ahmad ibn Muhammad ibn Yahya—Muhammad ibn al-Azhar—Muhammad ibn 'Abdullah al-Basri—Ya'la ibn Maymun—Yazid al-Zaqqashi—Anas ibn Malik (r.a.a.), the Messenger of Allah (s.a.w.s.) said: "When one brings joy with his words into the life of a believer or satisfies his worldly needs, whether small or large, it becomes an obligation upon Allah to offer him a servant on the Day of Last Judgment."

Respond to cruelty with kindness, and do not punish for an error. In a Hadith that comes through Muhammad ibn 'Abdullah ibn Muhammad ibn Sabih al-Jawhari—'Abdullah ibn Muhammad ibn 'Abdul-Rahman ibn Shiruyah—Ishaq ibn Ibrahim al-Hanzali—Qabisah—Sunayn—Abu Ishaq—Abu al-Ahwas: "Abu al-Ahwas's father asked the Messenger of Allah whether, if he were to go to a close friend and the man would not help him, he should do the same to the friend if he asked for help. The Messenger of Allah said no."

(1)   Do not find fault with your friends. Through Ahmad ibn Muhammad al-Bazari we learn that the Messenger of Allah said: "If you start seeking faults in Muslims, you will cause dissent among them or you will at least start dissension."

(2)   A follower of Futuwwah may go to a close friend's house without invitation. 'Abdullah ibn Muhammad ibn Ziyad

reports that Abu Hurayrah said: "One day when Abu Bakr and 'Umar were together, the Prophet (s.a.w.s.) came and asked, 'What are you doing here?' They answered, 'We swear by the One Who sent you as a true prophet that what brought us here is hunger.' Upon that, the Prophet said, 'Go to the house of such-and-such a man among those who have invited us to this city.' "

(3)   Do not find fault with food offered to you. We hear from Muhammad ibn 'Abdullah ibn Muhammad ibn Sabih that Abu Hurayrah said: "The Messenger of Allah never looked down upon any food presented to him. He ate it if he had appetite and did not eat it if he had no appetite."

(4)   Maintain good conduct and behavior, the kind that reflects the perfect behavior of the people of Paradise. We heard through Abul-Qasim Ibrahim ibn Muhammad al-Nasrabadhi that Anas (r.a.a.) was ill. A friend of his came to visit him. Anas said to his servant, "Serve whatever we have to our brother, even if it is a piece of bread, because the Messenger of Allah (s.a.w.s.) said, 'Generosity is a characteristic of the people of Paradise.' "

(5)   Follow the example of our Prophet in this station. We hear through Hafiz Muhammad ibn Muhammad ibn Ya'qub that the Prophet (s.a.w.s.) said: "To visit each other for Allah's sake is generous behavior."

The host should serve everything he has to his brother. Even if he has only a drop of water left, he should serve that. If he does not offer what is possible for him to offer, his day and night are under the curse of Allah.

(6)   Let there be familiarity and closeness among brethren. Through Muhammad ibn Muhammad ibn Ya'qub al-Hajjaji, we learn that the Messenger of Allah (s.a.w.s.) said: "The

believer is the one with whom one can be close. The one who is not close and the one to whom one cannot be close are of no use. The good among men are those from whom others profit."

(7)   Above all, be generous. Through Abul-Husayn ibn Sabih we find that 'A'ishah heard the Messenger of Allah (s.a.w.s.) say: "Paradise is the home of the generous."

(8)   Maintain old relationships. In a Hadith that comes to us through Muhammad ibn Mahmud al-Maruzi al-Faqih, 'A'ishah said that she heard the Messenger of Allah (s.a.w.s.) say: "Allah approves the keeping of old friendships."

(9)   Keep your friends' interest at heart and care for your neighbors. We learn through Ibrahim ibn Muhammad ibn Yahya that Ibn 'Abbas (r.a.a.) brought a gift to Ibn al-Zubayr, who said: "Someone who eats while his next-door neighbor is hungry is not a believer."

(10)   When you bring a gift of food that in turn is offered to you, you must be extremely careful of your manners. We hear through Ibrahim ibn Ahmad al-Abzari that the Messenger of Allah (s.a.w.s.) said: "Don't count your friend's mouthfuls."

(11)   In affairs that are not clearly sinful, be lenient with your friends. Through Isma'il ibn Ahmad al-Khallali we hear that the Messenger of Allah said: "The first sign of intelligence is to believe in Allah. The next is to be lenient with people in affairs other than the abandoning of Truth."

(12)   Get along with friends and help them. Through Isma'il ibn Ahmad al-Khallali we hear that Abu Sa'id al-Khudri (r.a.a.) said: "A man prepared a feast for the Messenger of Allah and his companions. When the food was brought to them, one declined to eat, saying that he was fasting. The Messenger of

Allah (s.a.w.s.) said, 'Your brother has invited you; he went to a lot of trouble for you. Eat now. You may make up your fast later.' "

(13)   Care for your brethren more than you care for your own family. Through Isma'il ibn Ahmad al-Khallali we hear that Fatimah, daughter of the Messenger of Allah, asked her husband, 'Ali (r.a.a.), for a servant. 'Ali answered: "Do you wish me to abandon those who have given up everything for Allah so that their bellies contract from hunger while I get you a servant?"

(14)   Permit your friends to claim your possessions as if they belonged to them. Through Muhammad ibn 'Abdullah ibn Zakariyya we learn that the Prophet (s.a.w.s.) used to use the property of Abu Bakr as if it were his own.

(15)   Invite guests, offer feasts, and be hospitable. Through Muhammad ibn Quraysh, we hear that the Prophet said, "How awful is a society that does not accept guests." And we hear through Muhammad ibn 'Abdullah that the Prophet (s.a.w.s.) said that there is no good in the one who does not welcome guests.

(16)   Respect your friends and show your respect for them. We hear through Isma'il 'Abdullah al-Mikali that Wathilah ibn al-Khattab al-Qurashi said that a man entered the mosque when the Prophet (s.a.w.s.) was alone. The Prophet got up to show him respect. When the man protested, the Prophet responded that to be paid respect is the right of the believer.

(17)   Be truthful. Abu 'Amr Muhammad ibn Ja'far and Ibn Matar and Muhammad ibn Ibrahim ibn 'Abdah declared that 'Urwah (r.a.a.) said that Sufyan ibn 'Abdullah al-Thaqafi asked the Messenger of Allah to teach him so that he need never ask anyone again. The Messenger of Allah answered, "Say that you believe in Allah; then always be truthful."

40

18)   Be satisfied with little for yourself, and wish much for others. Through Abu Bakr al-Diwanji we hear that the Prophet said, "The best of my people will enter Paradise not because of their achievements, but because of the Mercy of Allah and their quality of being satisfied with little for themselves and their extreme generosity toward others."

19)   Be kind and gentle to others. Through Abu 'Amr Muhammad ibn Ahmad ibn Hamdan we hear that Abu Sa'id al-Khudri said, "In an expedition with the Messenger of Allah, we saw a man riding a camel. He was rushing about, hitting people right and left. The Prophet said, so that the man could also hear, 'Whoever has an extra riding animal should give it to someone who has none. Whoever has extra food should give it to those who do not have any.' Then he started counting people's luggage. We all felt that none of us had any right to extra property."

20)   Love each other and frequent each other for Allah's sake. Through Muhammad ibn 'Abdullah ibn Sabih we hear that Allah Most High said through his Prophet (s.a.w.s.): "The ones who love each other for My sake deserve My love; the ones who give what comes to them in abundance deserve My love. The ones who frequent and visit each other for My sake deserve My love."

21)   It is most rewarding to love the lonely and poor ones and care for them. Through 'Abdullah ibn Muhammad ibn 'Ali ibn Ziyad we learn that 'Abdullah ibn 'Amr heard the Prophet say: "The people whom Allah loves best are His poor and lonely servants." Somebody asked, "What is their state, O Messenger of Allah?" He answered, "They are the ones who have nobody and nothing but their religion. On the Day of Last Judgment they will be brought to Jesus, the son of Mary."

(22)   Keep your word and what is entrusted to you. We learn through 'Abdullah ibn Muhammad al-Simidi that 'Abdullah ibn 'Amr heard the Messenger of Allah say: "If you have these four things, it does not matter even if you lose everything else in this world: protect what is entrusted to you, tell the truth, have a noble character, and earn your income lawfully."

(23)   Do not wear the garb of the Sufi before you have qualified for it by cleansing your heart. We learn through 'Abdullah ibn Ahmad al-Shaybani that al-Hasan (r.a.a.) heard the Messenger of Allah say, "Do not wear the woolen mantle of total devotion until your heart is clean, because if you wear these clothes while your knowledge is deficient, [Allah in His Name] al-Jabbar, the Compeller of the Heavens, will tear them off your back."

(24)   Give elaborate feasts, be gracious when entertaining, and be generous to your guests. Through Muhammad ibn al-Fadl ibn Ishaq and Abu Hurayrah (ı.a.a.) we hear that the Messenger of Allah said, "Whoever believes in Allah and the Day of Last Judgment, let him be gracious to his guests."

(25)   During these gatherings, begin your own meal only after everyone else has started eating. Muhammad ibn Ya'qub al-Asamm reports that the father of Ja'far ibn Muhammad said, "Whenever the Prophet (s.a.w.s.) ate with others, he was the last one to begin eating."

(26)   Understand that what you really own is not what you keep of your property, but that which you spend for your brethren. It is reported through 'Abdullah ibn Muhammad ibn 'Ali and 'Amr ibn Shurahbil that 'A'ishah recounted that someone presented a lamb as a gift to the Messenger of Allah. He distributed the meat. 'A'ishah said, "Only the neck is left for us." The Prophet said, "No, all of it is left for us except the neck."

27)   Share the joy of your brethren to the extent that if you are
keeping a nonobligatory fast, you will break it to join the
feast and festivities. Muhammad ibn 'Abdullah ibn Muhammad ibn Quraysh reported that Nafi' reported that Ibn
'Abdullah heard the Prophet say, "If a person who is fasting
joins his brethren and they ask him to break his fast, he
should break it."

28)   Know happiness and joy in your relationships with your
brethren. 'Abdul-'Aziz ibn Ja'far of Baghdad reports that al-
Husayn ibn Zayd said to Ja'far ibn Muhammad, "Tell me, did
our beloved Prophet ever joke?" He answered, "Allah
bestowed on him the best manner of joyfulness. Allah sent
other prophets who had suffering and distress, but He sent
Muhammad (s.a.w.s.) for mercy and compassion. One of the
signs of his kindness and love for his people was that he joked
with them. He did this so that they would not stay away from
him out of awe. My father, Muhammad, told me that his
father, 'Ali, was told by his father, al-Husayn, that he heard
the Messenger of Allah say: "Allah hates those who make
disagreeable and sad faces at their friends."

Remember that you are a servant of Allah and should not
regard yourself and your actions highly, nor should you
expect a return for your actions. We hear from Muhammad
ibn 'Abdullah al-Razi that someone asked Abul-'Abbas ibn
'Ata', "What thing most attracts Allah's anger?" He replied,
"When one considers himself and his actions highly, and
worse still, expects a return for his good deeds."

Repent ceaselessly, with the strongest will not to return to
the thing of which you repent, for only then is the repentance
acceptable. Through Mansur ibn 'Abdullah al-Harawi we hear
Abul-Hasan al-Muzayyin say, "Three things make repentance
real: regretting the past, deciding firmly not to return to the

43

state of which one repents, and having fear in one's heart. One is afraid because one knows perfectly well when one sins, yet does not know if one's repentance is going to be accepted or refused."

By loving the ones whom Allah loves, you attract His love to yourself. We hear through 'Abdul-Wahid ibn Bakr al-Warthani and Qannad Abu Musa al-Dabili that Abu Yazid al-Bistami said that a man asked him, "Show me the shortest way to reach Allah Most High." Abu Yazid said, "Love those beloved of Allah and make yourself lovable to them so that they love you, because Allah looks into the hearts of those whom He loves seventy times a day. Perchance He will find your name in the heart of the one He loves; then He will love you, too, and He will forgive you your wrongdoings."

(29)   You must also repent for the sins of your friends and not blame them for their faults. Abul-Faraj al-Sa'igh reports that the father of 'Imran ibn Musa al-Dabili recounted that Yusuf ibn al-Husayn came to Abu Yazid al-Bistami and asked him, "With whom should I associate?" Abu Yazid said, "Associate with a person who will come to visit you when you are ill and who will pray that you are forgiven when you do wrong," and he recited a couplet:

We come and ask about your health when you are sick.
We pray for your repentance when you sin.

(30)   Do not be idle, but work in this world until you reach the definite state of trust in Allah. As reported through Abu Bakr al-Razi and Abu 'Uthman al-Adami, Ibrahim al-Khawwas said, "It is not right for a Sufi not to work and earn his livelihood unless his situation makes it unnecessary, or he is clearly

ordered to abandon worldly work. But if he needs to work and there is no reason for him not to work, he must work. Withdrawing from work is for those who have attained a spiritual level at which they are freed from the necessity of possessions and the following of custom."

(31)   It is necessary to establish faith and trust between yourself and your Creator so that it is manifest in your state and your manners. Abu Hamzah says, "Although I totally trust in Allah and with this trust I intend to cross the desert hungry and without food, if my hunger does not become my food, I will be ashamed before my Lord."

(32)   Abide by the prohibitions of Allah. 'Abdullah ibn Marwan dropped a penny into a dirty well by mistake. He paid thirteen dinars to some workers to recover the penny. When he was asked to explain this curious action, he said that the Name of Allah was written on the penny. In respect for His Name, he had to retrieve the penny from the dirt.

Treat people as you wish to be treated. As the Prophet (s.a.w.s.) said, "As you wish people to come to you, go to them."

(33)   A man came to Ibn Yazdaniyar and said, "Give me some advice." Ibn Yazdaniyar said, "Judge others as you wish to be judged."

Take refuge in Allah with your essence and heart. The order comes from the Most High:

So [Lot] believed in Him and he said, "I am fleeing to my Lord; surely He is the Mighty, the Wise." (Koran 29:26)

(34)   Abu Bakr al-Tamastani has said, "Whoever among us

abides by the Holy Book and the Traditions of the Prophet, and knows himself and the world and the people therein, and with his essence and heart takes refuge in Allah sincerely and constantly, he will achieve his goal. But if he ever turns back to what he has escaped from, he will lose his purpose forever." The Messenger of Allah said, "Everyone's refuge is the place where he has taken refuge."

Be in contact with Allah or His Messenger or with the beloved ones who are close to Him. Abu 'Uthman al-Hiri said, "He whose relationship with Allah is sincere will read His Book carefully and thoughtfully, will hold His Words higher than all other words, and will follow the conduct and behavior ordered by Him. Whoever is sincere in his relation with Allah's Messenger will follow his Traditions, his direction, and his character, and will make him his guide in things to do and things not to do. He whose relation with those who are close to Allah is sincere follows their way and strives to acquire their habits and behavior. Those who fall from this state are among those who are destroyed."

Educate yourself to prevent preoccupation with the affairs of men, and direct your attention toward the Truth. Abu Bakr al-Tamastani relates: "Whoever strongly desires a sincere and direct relationship with Allah must know that this relationship will prevent him from preoccupation with worldly matters."

(35)   Have faith that your sustenance is guaranteed by Allah. Sahl ibn 'Abdullah says, "The one who is still concerned about his sustenance after the guarantee has been given to him by Allah, has no value for Allah."

(36)   Go along with friends and do not go against their wishes. Al-Musayyab ibn Wadih said, "If I tell one of my brethren,

'Get up, let's go,' and get the answer 'Where to?', I know that he is not my brother."

(37)   Do not oppose the one you love in things he likes or dislikes. Bishr ibn al-Harith said, "To like something that your beloved will disapprove of is not generosity," and he read a poem that said:

I still loved you, and I loved my enemies,
As my love for them was for you.
When you abased me, I abased myself;
How can I be kind to the one you find contemptible?

(38)   You must be very sensitive in following the rules of conduct in making your devotions and prayers to Allah. Sa'id ibn 'Uthman al-'Abbas relates that he went on the Pilgrimage eighty times on foot and in utter poverty. When he was circumambulating the Kaaba, there came to his heart a vast sense of love, and he uttered the words "O my beloved!" Then he heard a secret voice say, "Are you not yet prepared to give up your attachment to the feeling of love?" He fainted. When he returned to consciousness, he heard himself saying, "I am nothing, I am nothing, I am nothing."

(39)   The fine care given to the rules of conduct befitting Allah's perfect servant should not prevent him from being concerned about and protective of the interests of the public. Dhu Nun said, "The people of wisdom have three principles: to find peace within themselves, to spread the gifts of Allah in the company of the people who remember Him, and to inform men about Allah with a wise tongue."

(40)   Keep an accounting of your thoughts and deeds. For that, you have to be conscious and know yourself, and you must

have the conscience to regret that you are wasting your life in continuous revolt against your Creator. Al-Kattani says: "Someone from Raqqah told me that a man, in his attempt to keep an accounting of himself, had figured out that he was sixty years old. He counted the days, which totaled 21,500. He screamed in horror and fainted. When he came to, he said, 'Woe to me! Even if I had sinned only once a day, I would appear in front of my Lord with 21,500 sins. But I have sinned ten thousand times a day! What will become of me?' He passed out again. They tried to revive him and found that he was dead."

If Allah wills, the rest will follow.

PART TWO

In the Name of Allah, the Compassionate and the Merciful.

(1)   Retain the fear of Allah within and without yourself. Yahya ibn Mu'adh al-Razi has said, "There are two kinds of fear of Allah: the exterior fear, which secures your acting in this world only for Allah's sake, and the interior fear, which prevents you from receiving anything in your heart but Allah."

(2)   Fast, for hunger is a protection against the Devil. Ibn 'Isam says, "Whoever intentionally keeps himself hungry is out of bounds for the Devil."

Dhikr, or remembrance of Allah, will affect both your interior and exterior life. The effect of dhikr in the interior is acceptance (rida); in the exterior, its effect is humility and piousness (khudu' and khushu').

(3)   Junayd says, "Allah's servants are such that when they remember His magnificence, their limbs become paralyzed with anxiety at the thought of being separated from their Creator and from fear of their Lord. They are intelligent people who know Allah and the times that belong to Allah, and they are eloquent."

You must trust the security that Allah has granted you and work in accordance with His orders. Abul-Husayn al-Farisi says: "Do not think about your sustenance, which is secured for you, but do the work you have taken upon yourself. This is the way of the *fata* and of the generous."

(4)   None of the matters of this world or of the next should deter you from Allah. Rabi'ah said, "While I am in this world, all I want from this world is to remember You, and my only wish for the hereafter is to be able to see You. Other than this, do with me as You wish."

(5)   It is very important to take care of your members, limbs, and sense organs, and to safeguard them from evil. Use them properly to influence the education of your heart. Sahl ibn 'Abdullah al-Tustari has said, "Allah protects the hearts of those who protect their members from doing evil. No one whose heart is protected by Allah will be allowed by Him to feel insecure. Whoever receives Allah's security is transformed by Him into a leader who is followed by the people. Whoever is a guide appointed by Allah is made by Him into an example of perfection."

(6)   Forgive, even though you may have the power to retaliate. Sari says, "Whoever forgives while he has the power to take revenge is forgiven in his turn by Allah when he deserves punishment."

(7)   Instead of seeking the faults of others, look at your own faults. Dhu Nun has said, "Whoever looks for the faults of others is blind to his own faults. Whoever looks for his own faults cannot see the faults of others."

(8)   Strengthen your outer self with prayer and your inner self with remembrance of Allah. Yahya ibn Mu'adh said, "Allah created man's soul and made its life dependent on remembrance. Allah created man's flesh and made its life dependent on prayer. He created the world, and protection from its

dangers is possible only by abandoning it. He created the hereafter and made it possible to benefit from it only by working for it."

(9)   Be among the lovers who obey with pleasure all the wishes of the beloved. Abul-Husayn al-Maliki recounts that Nuri came to Junayd and said, "I hear that you give discourses on every subject. Speak to me on whichever subject you choose, so that I may add things that you do not know."

Junayd said, "What do you wish me to talk about?"

Nuri replied, "Love."

Junayd said, "Let me tell you a story. My friends and I were in a garden. One of us was supposed to bring our meal, but he was late. We went up on a terrace to look out for him. We saw approaching us on the path a blind man accompanied by a youth with a beautiful countenance. We heard the blind man say to the younger one, 'You ordered me to do "this." I did it. You prevented me from doing "that," and I did not do it. I have never acted against your wishes. What else do you want from me?' The young man said, 'I wish you to die.' 'Very well, I will die,' replied the blind man. He lay down and covered his face. I said to my friends, 'That blind man indeed looks lifeless, but he could not really have died; he must be pretending.' We came down, we looked at the man, we shook him and saw that he was indeed dead.'"

Nuri left without adding a word.

(10)   Be lenient with your friends, do not be cross with them, and do not talk harshly to them. Muhammad ibn Bashir tells of a quarrel between Ibn Sammak and a friend of his. At the end of the discussion, the friend said, "Let us meet tomorrow and continue this argument." Ibn Sammak answered, "No, let us meet tomorrow and forgive each other."

(11)   Respect others and be impressed only by the best in them. Junayd's dervishes complained to him about some people who kept asking him pointless questions. They requested him not to answer such people anymore. Junayd replied, "I do not see in them what you see in them. I hope that they will perchance fall on a word that they will understand and that one word will save them."

(12)   The masters of Futuwwah are told to give advice incessantly to their dervishes, but while they are preaching to them, they must never lose sight of the fact that many of the things that they ask of the dervishes are also missing in themselves. Badr al-Maghazili says that he asked Bishr al-Hafi, "What do you think about living in Baghdad?" and Bishr answered, "If you wish to die as a Muslim, do not stay here."

"Then why are *you* staying here?" Badr asked.

"If a servant ceases to follow Allah's commands, Allah throws him into a destructive and evil place," Bishr replied. "I must have stopped following Allah's commands, for He has thrown me here."

(13)   On the other hand, the novice must accept the words of his master even if he does not understand them, until the blessing of these words raises him to the level of understanding. On this matter, Junayd says, "I sat in the presence of sheikhs for ten years. They would talk about the wisdom of Sufism. I never understood what they discussed, but I never raised objections to their words. Every Friday I listened to their discourses. Although I did not understand a thing they said, I felt that it was true, and I prevented myself from falling into the cursed state of denial. After ten years has passed, they came to me one day and said, 'There is such-and-such a problem; if you have heard anything pertaining to a similar situation, tell us.' "

14)   Be compassionate, and prefer the interest of your brethren to your own egotism. According to the report of Muhammad ibn Hasan, Abu Ja'far al-Isfahani, who was Abu Turab's dervish, told this story: Abu Turab went to Mecca for the Pilgrimage. A man from Khurasan came to him. He had ten thousand dirhams in his possession. He opened the bag and said, "O Abu Turab, take this."

Abu Turab replied, "Pour it out."

The man from Khurasan poured the money onto the ground in front of Abu Turab. Abu Turab took two dirhams, gave them to one of his dervishes, and asked him to go and buy a shirt. Then he tore the shirt into shreds, making little bags out of them, and put handfuls of money in each. He then sent them to poor people, thus avoiding the embarrassment that would be caused by their having to come and ask for it.

When the money was almost distributed, a man reminded him that his own dervishes had not eaten anything for many days. Abu Turab took a handful of dirhams, gave it to him, and said, "Take this and feed them."

Then a woman approached. "O Abu Turab," she said, "what about your own family?"

Turning to his dervishes, Abu Turab said, "See if there is anything left." They searched on the ground, found two dirhams, and gave them to her.

(15)   In a tradition that comes to us through Muhammad ibn al-Hasan al-Baghdadi, Sari al-Saqati informs us of the following characteristics of the Sufis. They refuse to act for the fulfillment of their egos or to obtain anything that has a taste of willfulness, lust, pleasure, or whim. They are able to resist the commands of their egos. They firmly pursue five goals: never to be envious of what other people have, never to trouble other people, and always to control their hands, their

stomachs, and their sexual desires. They are humble and they follow the ones who are superior to them in mystical knowledge. They turn away from five evils: from everything that is temporal, from people, from desires, from the wish to be leaders, from the love of being praised. They wish for five gifts: that little of this world be given to them, but that Truth be given to them; that the fear of Allah be given to them; that the company of the ones close to Allah be given to them and that they be saved from the company of the ones who oppose Allah; that they be given the ability to know and do things that please Allah; and that they receive the things rejected by the ignorant.

(16)   To know Allah and to be able to endure pain and suffering for His sake is one of the main goals of Futuwwah. Abul-Faraj al-Warthani reports that Dhu Nun said, "One day, in Egypt, I saw some children throwing stones at a man. I asked the children what they wanted from him. They said, 'He is insane; he claims that he sees Allah.'

"I asked them to leave him alone and to let me see him. I approached and saw a young man leaning on a wall and told him, 'May Allah have mercy upon you. Do you know what these children say? They say that you claim to see Allah.'

"The young man did not answer, and kept quiet for an hour. Then he lifted his head, tears rolling down his cheeks. 'Allah is my witness that I have never lost Him since I came to know Him,' he said, and recited this poem:

"'O, from heights unreachable by us who are made
    of clay,
Blessings are sent.
This life is but a struggle;
The feet find their way only with death.'"

17)   When trouble and suffering come upon you, accept them and do not complain. 'Abdul-Wahid ibn Bakr reports that Muhammad ibn Mahbub said: "I was wandering in the streets of Baghdad. I passed through an insane asylum, where I saw a beautiful young man with shackles on his ankles and around his neck. I was so pained at this sight that I turned away from him. He called after me by name: 'O Ibn Mahbub, your Lord has put these shackles around my neck and on my feet because I love Him so. Is He not satisfied yet? Tell Him that if He is pleased, I do not mind this state of mine.' Then he recited this poem:

"'The one whom You brought close to You cannot stand to be away from You.
The one who is caught by love cannot stand to be away from You.
If the eyes cannot see You, the heart does.'"

(18)   Seek a humble life and poverty, and be content and happy with it. We learn from Abul-Faraj al-Warathani that Bishr ibn al-Harith said, "So Allah considers martyrdom a hidden pearl and offers it only to his most beloved servants. In the opinion of the believers, poverty is also such a hidden pearl."

(19)   It is detestable to fawn over and flatter someone in order to gain favor. 'Abdul-Wahid ibn Bakr reports that Abu 'Abdullah al-Qurashi said, "The one who flatters his own or someone else's ego will never smell the perfume of sincerity."

(20)   Free yourself from everything with which you find yourself surrounded, even from the whole universe, so that you may become a true servant of Allah. 'Abdul-Wahid ibn Bakr reports that Ahmad ibn Hanbal said that he saw a letter

written by Ibn al-Sammak to his brother. It said, "If you can, try to avoid being a slave to anyone but Allah, keep yourself free from submitting to worldly things, and be a servant to Allah alone."

(21)   In this education you must learn to feel joy in the privilege of serving your master. Ahmad ibn Muhammad ibn Ya'qub reports that Yahya ibn Mu'adh said: "Whoever feels joy in serving Allah will see that the whole material world will take joy in serving Him. The eyes that shine with the light of Allah will give light to the eyes that look upon them."

(22)   Concern yourself only with your own affairs; this also is a part of your education. Hafiz Abu Ahmad reports that the Messenger of Allah (s.a.w.s.) said: "One of the signs of a good Muslim is that he leaves alone everything that does not concern him." Ahmad ibn Muhammad Ya'qub reports that

(23)   Ma'ruf al-Karkhi (r.a.a.) said, "When a believer occupies himself with things that do not concern him, it is a sign of Allah's wrath upon him."

It is not sufficient to seek a humble life and poverty. You must also abide with the proper conduct in poverty. Through Mansur ibn 'Abdullah we learn that Abul-'Abbas ibn 'Ata said, "It is not proper to have anything more than the four things found on the table of the poor: the first, hunger; the second, poverty; the third, humiliation; the fourth, thankfulness."

(24)   When you speak, take care to speak only from your own experience and your own state. You should not talk about things you have not lived. Abu Bakr Muhammad Ja'far reports that Junayd said: "I traveled to the banks of the Euphrates, for I had been told that a *fata* lived there. I saw that the troubles of the whole world had gathered upon this noble man. I said, 'May Allah be pleased with you. Tell me, when does loyalty become perfect in this world?'

"He said, 'Junayd, the beginning of loyalty for you is not to ask this question.'

"I was hurt by his answer. He called me back and said, 'Junayd, to talk about loyalty without having lived loyally is not the kind of thing that good people do.' "

25) Realize your revolt against your Lord, fear the consequences, and hold on to this state. Through Abu Bakr al-Razi, we hear that Junayd said, "He is in grave error who takes into account the many good deeds that he has done when he sees a single offense in himself. If one does not follow Allah's orders in all sincerity, one is straying from the Truth."

26) Nothing and no one should prevent the servant from being in continuous remembrance of his Lord and from always enduring all troubles and pains. Muhammad ibn 'Abdullah ibn Shadhan reports that Junayd went early one morning to see Sari al-Saqati. Sari told him, "Abul-Qasim, tonight I was given a little inspiration, and my soul was told, 'O Sari, I created men and they were bound to Me and they were coming to Me. When I showed them the world, nine-tenths of them became world-bound and one-tenth remained with Me. When I told them about Paradise, nine-tenths of those who remained desired Paradise and only one-tenth remained with Me. When I poured My troubles and My pains upon those who had stayed with Me, they cried for help, and nine-tenths left and one-tenth remained with Me. I told them, "You neither wanted the world nor Paradise, nor did you run away from My troubles and pain." They said, "You know what we desire." I said, "I will pour upon you such calamities that the mountains could not bear their weight." They said, "As long as they come from You, it is well with us." ' "

27) Be aware of your states, count each breath and every moment of time allotted to you, and do not waste it. Sahl ibn 'Abdullah al-Tustari said, "Your time is the most valuable

thing you have. Give every moment its due." Abu Sa'id al-Razi reports that Junayd said: "All good is gathered in three conditions. If you cannot pass your days with what furthers you, at least do not pass your days with what works against you. If you cannot befriend good people, at least do not keep company with bad people. If you cannot give away what is yours for Allah's sake, at least do not spend your fortune on things that will anger Him. Keep continuous repentance and doubt that your repentance is accepted." Abu Bakr al-Razi reports that Abul-Hasan al-Muzayyin said, "Three things constitute repentance: regretting the past, deciding absolutely to give up what one has done, and fearing one's sins, because one may know one's sins intimately, but can never be sure that one is forgiven."

Hold on to Truth under any circumstances, and do not believe in the reality of circumstances. Abul-Hasan ibn Qatadah al-Balkhi reports that al-Qannad heard this story: Junayd was asked, "What are the attributes of the Sufis?" He answered, "They are such noble men that they keep their word." He was further asked, "How do you recognize them?" and answered, "They never close their eyes, so their hearts never fall into heedlessness and imagination."

(28)   Seek the company of the good and avoid the company of the evil. 'Abdullah ibn Muhammad ibn Isfandiyar reports that Yahya ibn Mu'adh al-Razi said: "On the day when the trumpet is sounded, you will see how evil friends will run from each other and how good friends will turn toward each other. Allah Most High says, 'On that day, except for the true believers, friends will be enemies.'"

(29)   Seek and pray to obtain wisdom in your knowledge, revelation in your wisdom, and witnessing of the Divine

Essence in your revelation. Yet you should also know that you will never attain the true knowledge of Allah in its entirety. Abul-Hasan ibn Qatadah al-Balkhi reports that Nuri said: "Allah made formal knowledge available to all people. To the ones close to Him He offered inner knowledge. To the ones who are pure, He offered His revelations. To the ones whom He loves, He permitted the witnessing of His Divine Essence. He hid Himself from all of His creation. Whenever they think they know Him, they are in confusion. When they think that the veils are lifting, they become veiled. When they think that they see, they become blind. I swear in the Name of Allah Most High that His doings are most strange. There is nothing stranger than His doings."

Do not be attached to worldly things. 'Ali ibn 'Abdullah al-Basri reports that Faris ibn 'Abdullah knew an old servant of Sahl. When she became ill, they proposed to have her cured. She refused. "Even if I knew that I would become totally cured by just having someone touch my ear," she said, "I would not let him do it. Where we are going is to our Lord; what a beautful voyage it is!"

(30) Believe that the one who loves receives constancy, health, and happiness from the Beloved. Sa'id ibn Muhammad al-Shashi reports that Sumnun al-Sufi said, "For you I have cried tears of blood. My tears became my cure." Muhammad ibn Isma'il recited this poem by a Sufi:

They thought that consummated love would quench
   desires
And love from afar extinguish ecstasy.
We tried both cures, yet have not found health.
Perchance it is better that your home be close, not far.

Receive the one who comes and do not run after the one who turns his back on you. 'Abdul-Wahid ibn 'Ali reports that Faris said, "In accordance with their ethics, the Sufis do not reject those who come to their door, and do not pursue those who do not come; nor do they try to dominate the ones who enter their circle."

A novice should not be rejected because of his faults nor a stanger accepted because of his good deeds. Abu Turab al-Nakhshabi has said: "When someone makes an effort to attain good behavior, takes on the outward form of the Sufis, and enters their circle, do not reject him, even if he commits one hundred faults. But do not let one who seeks the benefits of this world enter the circle without testing him, even if one hundred good deeds and benefits come from him."

(31)   It is important to assume the behavior of servantship. Through Husayn ibn Yahya we hear Junayd say, "To be a servant is to leave one's will, to be humble and modest."

(32)   Familiarity with friends visited or visiting must be understood. 'Abdullah ibn 'Ali al-Sarraj records Bishr ibn al-Harith as saying: "Among brethren, to leave the formality of good manners is good manners. He who is not familiar with his friends in activities permissible by Allah will bore them."

It is necessary to go beyond and in depth in one's efforts. 'Abdullah ibn 'Ali reports that al-Duqqi said: "One day 'Abdullah al-Kharraz came to visit me. I had been fasting for four days. He looked at me and said, 'A man goes hungry for four days, so hunger shouts at him and calls to him.' Then he said, 'Do you know that to obtain what you want from Allah, you must surrender every breath you breathe? Is that too much?'"

(33)   Listen and be respectful and humble in the presence of

people who remember and call upon Allah, and accept Truth from the tongues of those who preach it. Abul-Fadl Nasr reports that Fayd ibn Ishaq heard someone ask al-Fudayl ibn 'Iyad, "What is Futuwwah?" He answered that it is remembrance of Allah and humility in the presence of those who are devoted to Him, and that to follow Futuwwah is to hear and accept the truth from those who preach it. Abul-

(34) Fadl Nasr also reports that Waki' said, "One should be permissive toward the faults of one's friends and should not be envious of what they possess."

(35) Trust in Allah and seek help only from Him and not from the people whom He has created. Nasr ibn Muhammad reports that Yahya ibn Mu'adh al-Razi said: "Four qualities characterize those who are close to Allah: They trust in Him in all matters, they ask only from Him, they seek only His help, and they keep only Him in their hearts, to the exclusion of everything else."

(36) Show compassion to all Creation. Nasr ibn Muhammad reports that Junayd related that there was a sheikh in Damascus called Abu Musa al-Qumasi who was a man of Futuwwah; everyone praised him. One day, the sheikh's house collapsed on top of him and his wife. When people began to dig in the ruins, they found his wife first. "Leave me," she said. "Go and try to find the sheikh and save him. He was sitting in a corner over there." They left the woman, dug where she had pointed, and found the sheikh. "Leave me," he said. "Go and save my wife." Each wanted the other to be saved. That is the state of those who are together for the sake of Allah and who are friends and brothers in the name of Allah. They are in that compassionate state at all times.

(37) The one on the path of Futuwwah, if he is well-to-do,

should never for any reason take advantage of a poor person's services. Mansur ibn 'Abdullah al-Khawwas told a congregation how Junayd and his followers were once in a state of need. A well-to-do friend came upon them and saw on their faces the signs of hunger. The rich man asked one of the poorer dervishes to go with him to the market. He bought food, but made the poor dervish carry it. When they approached the mosque where Junayd and his brethren were waiting, Junayd called to them, "Throw away what is in your hands." None of them ate the food. Then the man who had bought the food was told, "How important the world must have become for you, that you make a poor man a porter for your sustenance.!"

Know that the One who gives and the One who takes is Allah, so do not abase yourself by asking things from others. Mansur ibn 'Abdullah al-Harawi recites from a poem by Ibn al-Rumi:

I see no one who can grant what Allah has not given
And no one who can stop the granting of what He gave.
Generosity, tolerance, and the giving of gifts belong
    to the Forgiving One,
So ask from Him alone.

The one who lowers himself and begs from any other besides Allah, may he be in greater need. A true man gives without being asked; whoever gives when begged from is no man. Allah curses those who bow before such misers.

Know that you are lacking in every sense, and do not be pleased with your state. Mansur ibn 'Abdullah reports that Abu Ya'qub al-Nahrajuri said: "The sign that someone is well guided by Allah is that he is aware of his lack of sincerity, his heedlessness in his remembrance of God, his lack of loyalty, and he is dissatisfied with this state. His intentions and efforts show that his need for Allah is ever-increasing, until the point where he gives up all desires.

All thanks are due to the Lord of Creation. May Allah bless and have mercy on our Master Muhammad and upon all his family, offspring, companions, and friends.

If Allah wills, the third part will follow.

PART THREE

In the Name of Allah the Compassionate and the Merciful.

(1)   Nothing in this world is worth discord between brothers. Mansur ibn 'Abdullah reports Muhammad ibn Suqah's account of two men who became brothers in religion. One of the men asked the other to give him something; the second man denied him, but the petitioner did not seem to mind. "My brother," said the second man, "you asked me for something and I did not do it. Why did you not care?"

"I have become your brother, and grew to love you long before I asked you this favor," answered the other man. "As long as my reason for loving you does not change, my attitude will not change, whether or not you give me what I asked for."

The other man replied, "I refused what you asked for only to try you. Now you can take whatever you wish from me. You have the same right as I do to what I own."

(2)   Ja'far al-Sadiq was once asked, "What is Futuwwah?" He replied: "Futuwwah is not possible with quarreling and backbiting. Futuwwah is feeding people, giving to them, being pleasant and honorable to them, and not causing them difficulties."

One of the necessities of Futuwwah is to abide with the

outer and inner codes of good behavior. Abul-Husayn al-Farisi reports that Abu Muhammad al-Jurayri said: "Religion possesses ten treasures—five outer and five inner. The outer treasures are to be truthful in your speech, generous with your property, and humble in your appearance, and to avoid causing difficulties to others, while bearing the difficulties caused by them. The five inner treasures of religion are to fear separation from Him, to wish to be with Him, to regret your wrongdoings, to have conscience, and to feel shame (hayya') before your Lord."

To lower one's state by making demands upon other people is ugly. Abul-Husayn al-Farisi relates that Abu Bakr Muhammad ibn Ahmad ibn Dawud al-Balkhi said: "The love of someone who does not cause difficulties is of long duration. To have a relationship with a friend who is shy and timid is pleasurable; but friends who have continuous needs and demands are unbearable."

Leave all your wants and desires in order to protect yourself from disasters. Al-Husayn ibn Yahya reports from Abu Turab al-Nakhshabi that "the avoidance of disasters depends on one's not responding to the desires of one's ego."

Trust only in Allah in order to be satisfied with what you have. Abul-Husayn al-Farisi reports from Abu Muhammad al-Jurayri that Junayd said: "Allah has taken it upon Himself to satisfy the needs of His Creation and to provide for its sustenance. That is why men of Allah have found peace in trusting Him, and in not wishing or accepting anything other than what He gives. The pure in heart who have attained union with Truth, after having achieved this trust in their Guide which abolishes doubts from their hearts, must not ask things from others, for to do so is a very ugly act."

(3)   Solitude and isolation are preferable to indiscriminate
mixing with people. 'Abdullah ibn Muhammad ibn Isfandiyar
reported in Damghan that Yahya ibn Mu'adh said: "Everything has a fortification around it, which protects it. The
castle of the being is isolation and the abandonment of the
society of people, because if someone is not with you, he will
be against you; the helpers are few and the times are cruel.
Hurry before they destroy you through yourself."

A man asked Fath al-Mawsili to give him advice. He
answered, "Be by yourself, stay away from people; you will
thus protect your religion and your happiness."

In order to be able to strengthen the latter stages of your
path, make a great effort to solidify the early stages. Abul-
Husayn al-Farisi relates that ibn 'Ata' said: "One will never
attain the higher states if one does not make firm one's
relationship with God at the beginning. The duties that must
be perfected in the early stages are obligatory prayers, reading
of the assigned portions of the Koran in a state of purity,
holding firm to the intermediaries (sheikhs), and having a
strong will. God will offer the higher states to those who hold
fast to these duties."

Do not let any issue come between you and your secret
with Allah. Abu Nasr al-Tusi reports that Abul-Faraj al-
'Ukbari related that Shibli asked him: "O Abul-Faraj, how do
you pass your time?"

"With my wife and children," he answered.

Shibli said, "So you spend your time, which is more
valuable than the philosopher's stone, with things other than
Allah? The Prophet (s.a.w.s.) says, 'Allah is jealous and loves
the jealous ones. He is jealous when anything other than His
love appears in the hearts of the ones whom He loves.'"

Abul-Faraj said, "I am jealous also."

Shibli said, "Man's jealousies are of people; Allah's jealousy is of time spent for anything but Allah."

To be able to see your own ego, act in opposition to its wishes. A wise man said, "When someone has a question about will and cannot find a guide to answer him, let him watch his ego's desires and do the opposite. Then the truth of the matter will be known."

To stand in the presence of Allah [qiyam] for Allah's sake, with Allah's help, and together with Him, is the goal. The sign of being in the presence of Allah for Allah's sake is that one's state is continuous and uninterrupted; one is not distracted even by miracles and higher states that may be granted, nor does one separate one's attention from Allah and hope for a reward. The sign of standing in the presence of Allah with His help and permission is one's effort to efface all material things, an effort that appears without one's own will and decision. The sign of being in the presence of Allah together with Him is the disappearance of everything other than Allah, in such a way that nothing hides Him or prevents one from being with Him.

The answer of Abul-Husayn al-Bushanji to a question about Futuwwah is significant. He said, "One of the principles of Futuwwah is to beautify one's essence with God: to love and want for one's friends the things that one loves and wants for oneself; in fact, to prefer one's friends to oneself, because Allah Most High says: 'But those who, before them, had homes [in Medina] and had adopted the faith, show their affection to those who came to them for refuge, and do not entertain in their hearts desire for things given to them, but give them preference over themselves, even though poverty was their [own lot] ' [Koran 59:9]. And the Prophet (s.a.w.s.) said, 'Your faith is not complete until you love for your brother that which you love for yourself.' "

One must understand the element of time and give importance only to time in time: that is, give immediate attention to time in the present, before it becomes the past. Sahl ibn 'Abdullah al-Tustari was asked, "When is the dervish saved from his ego?" He answered, "When he will not allow his ego to concern itself with any other time but the moment within which he is. That is when the Sufi will find peace."

Grace in behavior is a sign of Futuwwah. When Abu Sa'id al-Kharraz was asked what Futuwwah is, he answered, "To forget what one already knows, to show patience against the wishes of one's ego, to give up expectations from ordinary people, not to want, not to expect thanks and rewards, to be generous, to hide one's state, and to be modest."

Leave things in the hands of God. 'Abdullah al-Razi said that he read from the book of Abu 'Uthman that Shah ibn Shuja' said, "In order to put someone else in charge of something, one must abandon one's own will."

In generosity and benevolence, follow the example of Allah's Messenger (s.a.w.s.), who said: "Visit those who do not visit you, give to those who do not give to you, respond with kindness and good deeds to the harm that is done to you."

Seek good health, pray for it, and be thankful for it. Hazrat 'A'ishah asked the Prophet (s.a.w.s.), "O Messenger of Allah, if I find the Night of Power [when prayers are most accepted], what should I ask from my Lord?" His reply was, "Ask for forgiveness and health in this world and the hereafter."

(4)   Abu Bakr al-Warraq says, "The real health is in Allah's

forgiveness. Without His forgiveness, there is no health or well-being."

(5)   We learn from Abul-Husayn Muqsim that Ibrahim al-Khawwas said, "health and well-being are carried only by the prophets and by the saints." On that subject, Abu 'Uthman al-Maghribi says, "The sages among men are those who are able to communicate health and well-being."

Give all that you can and do not fall into the affliction of miserliness. The Prophet (s.a.w.s.) asked a man, "Who is your master?" He answered, "Al-Judd ibn Qays is my master, but he is a little stingy." The Prophet (s.a.w.s.) said, "Is there a worse sickness than miserliness?"

(6)   We hear through Abul-'Abbas al-Baghdadi that Ahmad ibn Masruq related that he was with Abu Nasr one day on the streets of Baghdad. All Abu Nasr possessed was a wrapper around his waist that was worth eight dinars. They were accosted by a beggar who asked alms for the sake of Muhammad (s.a.w.s.). Without a second thought, Abu Nasr took off his wrapper, folded it in two, tore off half, and gave it to the beggar. He took a couple of steps and then said, "My miserliness is despicable." He returned and gave the other half to the poor man.

(7)   Be content with little and accept your lot, so that you will not lower yourself in front of another. Through Muhammad ibn al-Hasan we hear Hasan al-Musuhi relate: "One day I was in the company of other people and all covered up because of the cold. Bishr ibn al-Harith came by and, seeing me thus, recited a poem:

" 'In the courtyard of worries and pain among people,
     night hides the day.

69

This is better for me than if tomorrow
Someone would say that I asked for goods from
   the living dead.
They asked, "Are you pleased with your lot?"
I said, "To be rich is to be content with little,
   not with property and wealth.
I am pleased whether I have or have not.
I only wish for the open path." ' "

(8)   Wish for the conditions that Sari al-Saqati enumerates. Through Muhammad ibn al-Hasan al-Khalidi we learn that Sari said that man's peace depends on five principles: avoid associating with evil people, be distant from ordinary people, and in this distance taste the taste of your own actions; at the same time, refrain from blaming or finding fault with people even to the extent of ignoring their rebellion against Allah. There are also five faults from which one should cleanse oneself: hypocrisy, argument, affectation, artificiality, and love of property and rank; and five curses from which one should free oneself: miserliness, ambition, anger, greed, and gluttony.

(9)   You can correct your state by correcting your actions. Abul-'Abbas ibn al-Khashshab reports that Dhu Nun al-Misri said: "The one who settles his affairs finds peace and comfort; the one who strives to come closer, comes closer; the one who keeps pure becomes cleansed; the one who trusts in God finds security; the one who mixes himself into affairs that do not concern him may lose the things that should concern him."

(10)   Humility is one of the requirements of Futuwwah. To be humble is to accept the Truth and to be noble. Abul-'Abbas Muhammad reports that Ja'far ibn Harun related that Fudayl

was asked about humbleness. He said that humbleness was to submit to Truth, to be led to it, and to accept it from whomever one hears it from. When asked about Futuwwah, Fudayl said that one should be noble in dealing with people.

(11)   Prefer the well-being and comfort of your brothers over your own, and relieve them of their difficulties. Abul-'Abbas al-Makhrami reports that Muhammad ibn Abu Ja'far al-Haddad was on the path of resignation [*tawakkul*] for ten years. He worked hard in the marketplace, but did not even buy a glass of water for himself, nor did he use his daily pay to go to the public baths. He distributed it all to the poor people of Shunziyyah and other places. When night came, he went from door to door, gathering crumbs of bread with which to break his fast.

(12)   You should have little association and a great deal of patience with ordinary people, and be satisfied with the absolute minimum. 'Abdullah ibn Muhammad reports that Yahya ibn Mu'adh said: "To associate with ordinary people is a curse; to be patient with their ways is very difficult. If you feel the absolute need to associate with people, you should keep company with believers, talk with them, befriend them, and try to learn their state so that you can also be with them in the hereafter."

To be modest and not to show pride toward your brothers are requirements of Futuwwah. 'Ali ibn Muhammad al-Qazwini reports that Abul-Husayn al-Maliki said that a wise man remarked that pride only results in others looking down upon one and finding one unbearable.

When you begin a worthy task, complete the good deed and do not leave it half done. Sa'id al-Madani read this poem by Abul-Hasan ibn Abu Balgh:

When you start a good deed, it becomes an obligation to
   complete it.
A kindness promised has to be given.
Remember my need. These thankful hands will stay with
   you forever.
Stretch your hands, offer the thing that is good for me.
Helping hands are bejeweled necklaces.

Do not speak harshly to anyone. Abul-Qasim Ja'far ibn
Ahmad al-Razi said his brother Abu 'Abdullah saw Bunnan al-
Hammal go to an effeminate man and urge him to behave
rightly. The man told him, "Get away from me, and mind what
you have." Bunnan said, "What do I have?" The man
answered, "When you left your house to come to me, you
thought you were better than I; that is what you have, and that
is enough for you to be concerned with."

When the true followers of the path of Futuwwah speak on
their own, or tell what they have heard from their sheikh, let
it be in confirmation, not in negation. Abu Qasim al-Muqri
says, "The first blessing bestowed on faithful novices
entering the path of Sufism comes when they accept as true
that Allah has granted gifts to them and to their sheikhs, and
that miracles have been shown to them."

(13)   You must accept with grace the pains and troubles caused
by your friends and apologize for them. 'Ubaydullah ibn
'Uthman reports that ibn Masruq said, "Once I caused
trouble to Abul-Qasim al-Haddad. In response he wrote this
poem:

"If you try someone else, you will remember me
   and see what a treasure I am for you.

When you rose up, I remained humble.
I belonged to those who stayed small
  while their brothers gained favors.
You will regret what you did and throw away your
  lance,
And you will know that what you did was out of
  weakness.

"I went to him and said, 'I was not criticizing so that you should come and ask pardon, but because I saw loyalty in you.' "

Listen to good discourses, participate in good conversations, and abide by the prescribed behavior upon these occasions. Having good manners means showing respect to those who are superior to you; loving friendship and agreement to those who are your equals; kindness and compassion to those who are lower than you; obedience and modesty to your mother and father; and compassion in the education of children. It means caring for your womenfolk; visiting and doing good deeds for relatives; loving your brothers and eliminating all and everything that may prevent you from loving them; offering good-hearted smiles and generosity toward all humankind; knowing the values of the Sufis and respecting their rights; not showing any need toward the rich; accepting the knowledge from men who know; humbly obeying men of wisdom without negation; and fleeing from the dogmatic ones, heretics, profiteers, and men who wish to enslave others.

In relation to knowing the value of the Sufis, my grandfather told me that Abu 'Uthman said, "Whoever has self-respect shows respect to others, and whoever does not have self-respect has no respect for others."

Keep your friends' secrets and be loyal to them. Mansur ibn 'Abdullah reports that Rabi' al-Kamikhi told the following story in Ramla: "I was in the company of dervishes and had money with me. I took it all out and distributed it among them. My ego whispered to me, 'Keep one dirham for yourself,' so I kept one. Some days later, my appetite whispered, 'Get something to eat.' I went to the marketplace and gave the dirham to the shopkeeper. To my astonishment, I saw that the silver had changed into copper. The shopkeeper would not accept it, nor would anybody else in the marketplace. I went to my brother dervishes and said, 'O my friends, forgive me. I cheated you by keeping this coin.' One of them took the coin, went to the marketplace, and bought enough bread and grapes for all of us to share."

Expel all self-approval and pride from your being. Ibrahim al-Khawwas said, "Pride prevents one from knowing one's real value, as haste leads one away from Truth, and as gentleness and thoughtfulness prevent regret. All power belongs to Allah."

(14)   Behave toward your friends in a way that will prevent them from doing something for which they would have to apologize. 'Abdullah ibn Muhammad al-Damghani reports that Yahya ibn Mu'adh al-Razi said, "He who forces upon you a condition that necessitates apologies is not a friend. Neither is he a friend who does not offer you something before you ask for it."

Envy is a dreadful thing from which you must flee. Abul-Qasim Ibrahim ibn Muhammad al-Nasrabadhi reports that 'Abdul-Rahman ibn Abu Hatam said, "These are the signs of those on the path of Futuwwah: They do not envy others for the gifts that Allah bestowed upon them; they do not see the faults of others, as they fear that Allah may afflict them with a similar sin; they are pleased with Allah's judgment of their state, whether it is in their favor or against them."

A noble character that is expressed in action is a sign of this path. Al-Nasrabadhi tells of hearing a follower of the path say: "Nobility of character consists in holding to and acting upon Allah's Word in His Holy Book and following the example of His Prophet (s.a.w.s.)—being soft-natured and having a happy disposition, taking care not to mistreat others, and continuously doing good. Allah Most High chose His Prophet (s.a.w.s) on the basis of these sacred words: 'Take to forgiveness and enjoin good, and turn away from the ignorant!' " (Koran 7:199).

Abu Bakr al-Warraq says on this subject: "In the older days, the followers of the path used to praise their friends and abase themselves. Today they praise themselves and abase their friends. They used to choose good and comfort for their friends and harshness and a hard life for themselves. Now they choose a hard life and harshness for their friends and gifts and comforts for themselves."

(15)   Do not occupy the present with the preoccupations of the past and the future. 'Abdullah ibn Yahya reports that Yahya ibn Mu'adh said, "To worry about the affairs of the past and to be preoccupied with the affairs of the future takes the blessing out of life."

(16)   'Ubaydullah ibn Yahya relates that Yahya ibn Mu'adh said, "Three habits will ameliorate your character and your actions: Do not consider the rich your enemies, but look upon them as a lesson. Do not regard the poor with arrogance, but look upon them with humbleness. Do not gaze at women with lustful eyes, but look upon them with compassion and kindness."

Spend what you have on your friends. Abu Bakr al-Razi

75

reports that Muhammad ibn 'Abdullah al-Kattani said: "On the Day of Last Judgment, the servant of Allah will be asked a full accounting of his expenditures, with the exception of that which he spent on his friends, because Allah would be ashamed to ask for that."

(17)   Show compassion both to the ones who obey and the ones who rebel. Muhammad ibn 'Abdullah ibn Shadhan reports this story of Ibrahim al-Atrush: "We were sitting on the shores of the Tigris River with Ma'ruf al-Karkhi. A boat full of young people drinking and playing tambourines was passing by. One of the dervishes said, 'O Abu Mahfuz, do you see the ones who revolt against their Lord in that boat? Pray to Allah that they be cursed!'

Ma'ruf lifted his hands to heaven and prayed in this fashion: 'O Allah, my Lord, I beg you to make these people as joyful in heaven as you have made them joyful in this world.'

" 'But we asked you to curse them!' said one of his people.

"Ma'ruf answered, 'My brothers, if God accords them joy in heaven, it will be because He has accepted their repentance.' "

Know the value of your friends, and in their company forget all the good deeds you did for them. It is repeated by Abu Bakr Muhammad ibn 'Abdul-'Aziz that Abul-Qasim Ishaq ibn Muhammad said: "When I left Abu Bakr al-Warraq, I asked him to tell me with whom I should associate. He answered, 'With those who forget the favors they have done for you. Beware of those who remember the help they have given you, and remind you of it when they meet you. Also beware of those who value you according to their needs, which they expect you to satisfy.' "

Be more preoccupied with your inner state than with your external state, because the inner state is what Allah looks at, whereas the outward appearance is what people look at. Abu Bakr al-Razi reports that Abu Ya'qub al-Sufi said: "There are men who will devote fifty years of effort to guarding against the slips of the tongue in recitation of the Koran, yet are not at all mindful of the slips that their inner being makes. People in that state are misguided."

Be exceedingly conscious of your manners in social intercourse. Sahl ibn 'Abdullah advised: "Be just to your enemies and benevolent and loyal to your friends."

(18)   Keep your good manners even when you are by yourself, alone with Allah. Abu Nasr al-Isfahani reports that Abu Muhammad al-Jurayri said: "I have never sat with my legs stretched out when I was alone." Abu Bakr al-Razi reports that Abu Yazid al-Bistami related that he woke up one night, prayed, sat, and stretched his legs. He heard a voice saying, "Those who sit with a Sultan should sit with the proper manners."

(19)   The followers of the path are advised to keep old affections and relations. The Prophet (s.a.w.s.) says that Allah likes old friendships. Abu Bakr al-Razi reports that Abu Muhammad al-Maghazili said, "One who wants to continue to receive love and care should be faithful to his old affections and relationships."

Hide your states. Sahl ibn 'Abdullah said, "Five things express the beauty of a being: when the poor appear rich; when the hungry appear satisfied; when those with heavy hearts appear joyful; when love is shown to an enemy; when feebleness does not appear despite fasting the whole day and praying the whole night."

On the necessity of being continuously aware of one's outer and inner states, Abu 'Ali al-Juzajani said, "Consistency in this path depends on the heart being in constant agreement with Allah and the spirit in constant battle with the body."

Renounce the whims of your ego and your negative attitude. Do not let your ego's every wish lead you, because it can ony lead you into darkness; whims are created from darkness. Abide with your intelligence, because it will lead you to light, to the realm of Allah's attribute *al-Jabbar* (the All-Compelling).

Cleanse your being from revolt and beautify it with obedience to Allah. Abu 'Ali al-Juzajani said: "Decorate your ego with piety and fear of Allah. Cleanse it with consideration and fear; dress it up with conscience and love; then give it to the care of your Lord with submission and selflessness. Submit your ego to His Will, so that He will educate it and bring it up for you."

(20)   In order not to fall into calamity, save yourself from bad acquaintances. 'Abdullah ibn Muhammad ibn Isfandiyar declared in Damghan a saying of Yahya ibn Mu'adh al-Razi: "The more one mixes with bad company, the more one will fall into error. Whoever protects himself from bad company and their talk will be saved by Allah from empathizing with them and inclining toward their ways."

(21)   Be careful and stingy with your faith, and free and generous with your property. 'Abdullah ibn Muhammad Isfandiyar al-Damghani declared in Damghan that Yahya ibn Mu'adh al-Razi said: "The believer may be cheated out of his property, but never out of his religion. And while the religion of the hypocrite could easily be taken away from him, it is impossible to take away any of his property."

A follower of the path of Futuwwah will prefer his spiritual master over everything that he may possess in this world. Abu 'Ali al-Bayhaqi reports that Abu Bakr ibn Yahya al-Sufi tells the following story. The caliph al-Ma'mun came home one day and told his household, servants, and slaves that they could take whatever they wished from the contents of the house, and it would be theirs. Everyone ran to claim some valuable object. Only one slave did not leave the side of the caliph, not caring what was going on, just looking at his master.

"Why do you not also go and take something?" asked the caliph.

The slave replied, "Do you mean what you say, O Master of the Believers, that I may have for myself whatever I choose?"

"Yes," answered al-Ma'mun. The slave took hold of the caliph and said, "I want only you and nothing else." The caliph gave him much more than the others took, and from that time considered none equal to him.

All thanks are due to the Lord of the Worlds and all blessings and salutations to our Master Muhammad and his progeny.

PART FOUR

In the Name of Allah, the Compassionate and the Merciful; I put my trust only in Him.

A principle of Futuwwah is never to forget your brothers in the path. Abu Muhammad al-Jurayri said: "Loyalty to and consideration for others is a means to awaken consciousness from the sleep of heedlessness and to prevent thoughts from the disasters of imagination."

In your relationships with people, do not bow in front of men for the benefits of this world, and do not lower yourself by being condescending. Referring to this, Mu'awiyah ibn Abu Sufyan said: "The one who comes to you with a bowed head to ask for something, comes to you selling Allah's blessings bestowed upon him, and loses his dignity for the sake of your power."

The *qadi* [judge] Abu 'Ali al-Husayn ibn Ahmad al-Bayhaqi recites a poem of Muhammad ibn Hazim:

To wear clothes torn in two pieces
    and to be bent in hunger two nights and a day
Is better than to bow in need
    that closes the eyes with shame.

My family is numerous, my wealth next to nothing.
I still live with God's direct sustenance
And do not sell my dignity by asking from others.

My needs are between my Lord and myself,
  And no other than He will ever know.

Relations between brethren must be such that when they
see each other, their hearts should fill with joy. Isma'il ibn
Abu 'Umayyah said: "It should be easy to go and see a friend
among the brethren, and one should not hesitate to do so. Be
wise, see how important it is, and consider it a blessing and a
gift." Ibn Mubarak said, "To see one's brethren strengthens
one's faith, and is a cure for illness." Sufyan al-Thawri
declared that he had no other pleasure left in this world
except to be with friends.

Among brethren, all should do good deeds for each other
without being asked. Sa'id ibn al-'As said: "To really help is
to help without being asked. Even if you gave all you
possessed to someone who came begging for something and
was unsure whether you would give it or not, all that you
could give him would never equal what he had lost." In the
town of Kufa, Abu Dharr al-Mundhiri al-Warraq recited the
following line from a poem: "Allah's curse be upon him who
takes from the hand from which he begged in need."

You must also serve without being asked. Sufyan al-Thawri
said, "It is contrary to Allah's noble ethics not to serve when
you are able to serve." Al-Ma'mun said to al-Fadl ibn al-
Rabi': "Consider it a happy occasion when you are able to
provide help to someone in need, because you do not know
what the next moment will bring; destinies may change and

life may be so short that you may not complete an act nor see a joy mature."

Thus you should show graciousness to the needy and shy away from the rich and powerful. Al-A'mash reports that Abraham (s.a.w.s.) used to show joy at the coming of poor guests, and serve them with pleasure. But when rich and noble guests came to his house, he would serve them with shyness.

In your relationships, if you should encounter an insolent person, show understanding and forbearance; and if you should meet someone who does you harm, respond with forgiveness. Abu Bakr al-Mufid reports that the father of Muhammad ibn 'Isa al-Qurayshi heard a man advising his son in this manner: "Be gentle with those who are harsh with you; forgive those who cause harm to you. Always leave room for peace and harmony, so that your friends will come even closer to you and your enemies will be ashamed of what they did to you."

(1)   Show continuous love and understanding, and never leave your friends because of the inconvenience that they may cause. Sheikh Abu Sahl Muhammad ibn Sulayman reports that Ahmad ibn Yahya recited this poem:

A friend who meets you with a sour face
    and finds other friends when you leave
    is not a friend.

A friend is he who is ever united with me
    and keeps my secrets from everyone.

Abul-Fath al-Qawwas al-Zahid said in Baghdad, "One who

82

changes friends for no reason must have shown love only for
profit."

(2)   A follower of the path must have a high goal in both
spiritual and material matters. Muhammad ibn 'Abdullah al-
Razi reports that Junayd once said, "A person's value is
according to his intentions and aims. If someone's goal is the
worldly and the world, his value is nil. He whose goal is the
hereafter has a great value, as great as the Paradise between
the heavens and the worlds. The value of one whose sole
purpose is Allah's pleasure, is Allah's pleasure on earth and in
heaven. His value cannot be measured by any other means. As
Allah Most High says: 'Allah's pleasure is greater than
everything' " (Koran 9:72).

Abu Tayyib al-Shirazi said: "As I was leaving Abu Bakr al-
Tamastani, I asked him for advice. He said, "Try harder.""

Abu 'Ali al-Ja'fari al-Basri recited Isma'il ibn 'Abbad's
poem about his own state:

> They told me I was plagued with difficulties
> And my pain became the talk of the people.
> I said, "Leave me be with my pain and troubles,
> For a man's pain is in proportion to his effort."

Abu Ahmad al-Hiri reports these words of Abu 'Ali al-
Thaqafi: "Have noble aspirations, for it is aspiration, not ego,
that carries everything in this world. 'You have loaded on
your heart things the body cannot bear.' Your heart carries
what the body cannot."

Uphold these five virtues for the preservation of your
being: Keep safe what has been lent to you; protect and
preserve the good in yourself; be truthful and honest; be

patient, pure, and selfless toward your brothers; and seek the salvation of your soul. Whoever loses one of these virtues loses his aim. Some wise men have said, "The one who possesses these six qualities knows that he indeed possesses Futuwwah: He is thankful for the little that he has, patient amid the greatest trouble, kindly to the ignorant, and generous so as to educate the miser; he seeks no praise for doing good, and does not stop doing what he believes to be good out of fear of criticism." Yahya ibn Mu'adh said that Futuwwah is peace, generosity, loyalty, and modesty.

Abul-Hasan ibn Sam'un said that Futuwwah is not doing in secret that which would shame you if done openly. Abul-Husayn al-Maliki said: "Futuwwah is superior character and behavior, and inner purity."

Abu 'Amr al-Dimashqi said: "Futuwwah is considering other people's actions with tolerance while regarding your own with dissatisfaction; respecting the rights of those who are superior, inferior, or equal to you; and adhering to your friends despite their mistakes and wrongdoings, because when you love someone, his cruelty should incite your loyalty. The beloved's turning away from you should make you go toward him. Anger, either felt or expressed, should have no part in loving friendship; otherwise love is lacking, and the relationship depends only on interest."

Abu Sa'id al-Razi recites these lines of Ibn al-Anbari:

I will force myself to forgive all who have sinned,
    no matter how often and how much they have sinned.

Men are of three kinds only: noble men, men of honor,
    and men who endure.

I know to respect those who are above me, and raise
myself to truth. Truth is all that is necessary.

Kindness must be the judge of the faults and errors
of those who are my equals.

The wish of one who is less fortunate than I becomes
a matter of honor to me, no matter what others think
and say.

This is how I stand.

(3)   Love must be met by love, because the only response to
love is love. Abu Bakr al-Mufid reports that Ibn al-Mubarak
said: "Respond with pure love and follow in obedience those
who love you and think well of you."

Compassion must be the basis of your relationships in
Futuwwah. Junayd was asked about compassion toward
others. He answered, "Give them what they want, do not ask
them to do something that is beyond their capacity, and do
not tell them things that they will not understand." Someone
was asked the extent of his compassion toward his brothers.
He answered, "If a fly were to sit on my brother's face, I
would feel it on my own face," and he recited this couplet:

I am jealous of the earth upon which you walk.
O, I wish instead that you would walk on my face
    so long as I live.

Ruwaym was questioned about compassion. He answered,
"Know that I have no joy in this world other than my

brothers' joy. Neither do I feel any pain except the pain that my brothers feel."

Another follower of this path was asked about the love and compassion he felt for his brethren. He replied: "When I see them, I am sad that all my being is not one eye to see them, and I am jealous of my own eyes; and when my ears hear their voices, I wish that my whole being were an ear to hear their voices, and I am jealous of my ears." He added, "One night, Khidr* came to my house and sang to me, and I felt the same way about him—I wished that my whole being could hear him." A sheikh asked him, "How should one express one's wish for one's friends?" he answered, "One should be able to say: 'I have truly experienced that all my being became an ear to listen to them.'"

Someone read this poem:

In my care for you, I protect you from my own eye.
Perchance my sight hurts you; I close my eyes.
When I see you thinking about yourself,
I am jealous of your thoughts.
I am jealous of the angels on your two shoulders.
If I could, I would stop the words
   that caress your lips.

Another friend was asked about how much concern and love he felt for his friend. He said, "As long as I see him, I do not care to see anything else. As long as I hear his words, I do

* A guiding spirit existing at all times who appears in human form to help those worthy to be guided.

not care to hear anyone else." And he recited, "If I could, I would close my eyes to everything except you."

Another friend said: "During the days I was separated from my friends, the yearning for their presence made me deaf and dumb to all others. Do you know of such an affliction as being rendered deaf on account of your friends' absence?"

Leave all your preoccupation with yourself, with your own interests and needs, and take care of the dependents Allah has bestowed upon you. It is related that 'Abdullah ibn 'Umar forgot his own hunger but fed his slaves, and neglected his own clothes but dressed his servants well. In every way he preferred their needs to his own. He used to say that doing this was easiest for him, and that it was protection against the terrors of his ego.

In contrast, anger and negativity are evils that you should escape from. Mu'awiyah ibn Abu Sufyan said, "Why should I be angry about what I possess, and why should I be angry about what I do not possess?" If I have power, then I am able to put things right for myself; why should I get angry? If I have no power, what is the sense of my getting angry, as it will do no harm to my enemy?"

(4)   Know the value of time and how to act and behave in the present. Abul-Husayn al-Farisi reports that Junayd said, "The best deeds are done when a man knows the value of time. When he keeps his attention only on the demands of present situations, he prevents himself from overstepping the boundaries that Allah has assigned him; this also prevents him from following anyone but his Lord."

Muhammad ibn 'Ali al-Tirmidhi said, "No one but [Muhammad] al-Mustafa (s.a.w.s) was able to obey the rules of the right time and the right action. He said: 'I have

87

submitted myself to You, left my affairs in Your hands. None other is my support.' He also said: 'I take refuge in You from You.' Allah Most High in turn tells us about the presence of His Prophet (s.a.w.s.), beautifying him and praising him: 'And surely thou hast sublime morals' " (Koran 68:4).

(5)   See only good in your friends and, observing evil in yourself, know that you are far from good. This is the proper attitude for you. Abu 'Abdullah al-Sajazi said: "As long as you do not see your virtues, you are virtuous; if you see your merits, you have no merits." Abul-Husayn al-Farisi reports that Shah ibn Shuja' al-Kirmani said: "As long as they do not see their merit, the possessors of merit are virtuous. When they attribute virtue to themselves, their merits are canceled. Saints do not claim sainthood. The ones who claim to be saints, even if they were, are deprived of their sanctity." Shah ibn Shuja' asked Abu Hafs about Futuwwah. Abu Hafs answered, "Futuwwah is morals."

(6)

Sincerity felt and expressed outwardly toward your brethren is the basis of this morality. The governor Abu Ahmad al-Hafiz reports these words of a wise man: "One of the rules of the brethren is that they should love each other wholeheartedly, teach and educate each other with their words, aid each other with their property, straighten each other with their morals, and defend each other in their absence. Associate with those who are superior to you in your spiritual dealings and with those who are less fortunate than you in your worldly dealings."

'Uthman ibn Hakim said: "In religious associations, befriend those who are superior to you, and in worldy associations, befriend those who are inferior to you. Associating spiritually with people who are inferior to you will weaken your discipline and obedience to Allah. Associating in worldly affairs with people who are less fortunate than you will magnify Allah's gifts to you and strengthen your thankfulness."

Dawud al-Ta'i said, "Befriend the believers, because they, of all the people of this world, will give you the least trouble and the most help." Trust your Lord and hope only from Him. Sufyan ibn 'Uyaynah relates that someone asked Abu Hazim about the extent of his fortune. He answered, "I possess only two things: One is my trust in God, that I ask only of Him; the other is my lack of desire for what is in the hands of other people."

Have good wishes for your brothers, and show more kindness to your friends than to your relatives. Husayn ibn Yahya al-Shafi'i reports that Ja'far ibn Muhammad al-Sadiq said: "Whoever does not behave toward his brethren as he behaves toward himself is not paying brotherhood its due. Do you not see how God Most High, in His Holy Book, declares that the son will run away from his father and the brother [by birth] from his brother on the Day of Last Judgment? Then He indicates the compassion among friends by saying: 'So we have no intercessors, nor a true friend' " (Koran 26:100-101).

Protect every limb of your body and your inner being from sinning. Someone asked Abul-Hasan al-Bushanji to define Futuwwah. He answered: "It is preventing yourself from any action of which you would be ashamed if Karim and Katib, the two angels on your shoulders who record your deeds, would witness it."

Hudhayfah al-Mar'ashi said, "Futuwwah determines the right use of the eye, the heart, the tongue, and the desires. Prevent your eye from falling on anything unlawful; let your tongue speak only the truth; do not let your heart contain vengeance or treachery; do not let your desires lead you to wrongdoing.''

Abul-Husayn ibn Sam'un said: "Futuwwah means opposing and arguing little, being fair; preventing errors in oneself and not criticizing the errors in others; trying to correct one's faults; accepting accusations; enduring troubles caused by others; lowering one's ego; being pleasant to both the old and the young, doing good deeds, giving good advice, and accepting advice; loving one's friends, and bearing peacefully with one's enemies. These are the visible aspects of the path that are sufficient for us to know until we are able to hear and tell about the truths of Futuwwah.''

Your inner feelings and the outward expression of these feelings, your whole inner being, and your total appearance must be one and the same. Abu Dujanah reports that Dhu Nun al-Misri said, "A person who does in secret what he would be ashamed to do in public has no self-respect; in fact, he does not even consider himself a living being.''

To be good is to empty and cleanse your essence of the universe and all that it contains. Abul-'Abbas ibn 'Ata' says: "He who does not separate his spirit from the world, does not empty his soul of the people, and cannot remove his essence from the veils of his ego, cannot be one with his Lord. But he who can free his spirit from everything but Allah will receive many gifts, and he will know the difference between those who receive pleasure and blessings from their Lord and those who receive His wrath.''

Fear only your Lord, and you will need to fear nothing else. One of our ancestors told a wise man, "Why do you not buy some property so that you can later leave it to your children?" He responded, "That is not good advice. I might risk the consequences of possessing property for myself, but I prefer to entrust my children to my Lord; for them, I wish to leave my Lord as inheritance."

Follow the advice of your brethren rather than your blood relatives. Hafiz Abu 'Ali 'Umar recited the following poem in Baghdad:

> My spiritual brethren are no different to me
>   than my mother's sons.
> You may find me free, strong, and obeyed,
>   but I am a slave to my brethren.
> I separate good deeds done and gifts given,
> But join my consideration for my brethren
>   to what I am.

True hospitality and mutual respect are expressed in the following tale told by Abu Muhammad al-Jurayri: "Sheikh Ibn Masruq had invited us to his house. Along the way we encountered a friend and told him that we were invited to the sheikh's house but that we did not exactly know the way, and we asked him to take us there. He said, 'I was not invited; the sheikh might see me approaching his house with you.' Nevertheless he agreed to lead us so as not to oppose our wish. When we came to the sheikh's door, our friend stayed away. We told our host what had happened. The sheikh said, 'I thought that my place in his heart was such that he would feel free to come to my house without invitation. If I have offended him, he must step on my cheek.' We tried to convince the sheikh that it was not necessary, but he had made an oath. So we laid a clean cloth on the floor, and the sheikh placed the side of his face there. We lifted our friend by the arms so that his feet lightly touched the sheikh's face. Then he was made to sit in the sheikh's place."

Be very patient with your brethren, and do not change friends because of impatience. The prophet David told his son, the prophet Solomon: "Do not exchange an old and tested friendship for a new one. If you do, you will be changing one gift from Allah for another. Know that a thousand friends are too few, and even a single enemy is too many."

Someone complained to a wise man about difficulties in the affairs of business and property. The wise man answered, "My brother, do you wish a better caretaker than Allah?"

We must be patient with the way Allah has organized our lives. Someone said, "One who is impatient with the conditions of life that Allah has offered him is not going to be patient in letting Allah guide his spirit." Al-Wasiti said: "Whoever sees himself and everything else as belonging to Allah becomes one with Allah, and will not need anything else." Abul-'Abbas al-Dinawari said: "Whoever depends on himself alone will have regrets in the end. Whoever accepts what Allah has destined for him will be thankful to Allah both at the beginning and at the outcome of his affairs."

(7)   When elders or those who have a higher spiritual rank invite a young novice, they must serve him with pleasure and love. Hafiz 'Ali ibn al-Husayn reports that Yahya ibn Aktham said that he was once invited by the caliph al-Ma'mun. He became thirsty in the middle of the night and got up to fetch water. He heard the caliph say, "Why are you not asleep, O Yahya?" He answered, "I was awakened by thirst, O Commander of the Faithful." The caliph ordered him to return to bed, and personally brought a glass of water to him, saying, "Do you not know that for a host to ask his guest to

(8) help is not good behavior?" He then added that the brother of Caliph Harun al-Rashid related that the Prophet (s.a.w.s.) had said: "To make one's guest serve is a cause for shame."

If fate separates you from your brethren and friends, no joy is left in life. Al-Husayn ibn Yahya said that Ja'far ibn Muhammad told how Junayd was seen one day extremely sad and thoughtful. Someone asked him, "O Abul-Qasim, what distresses you?" He answered, "I lost my friends with whom I was close; I lost my being in seclusion; from there on the body is crushed and the heart is troubled." He recited the following poem:

After suffering the pangs of love
I have no place to go.
How empty it is
When the beloved is gone.

(9) Hafiz 'Ali ibn 'Umar recited the poem of 'Ubaydullah ibn 'Abdullah ibn Tahir:

If one were free to throw oneself away,
One would cast oneself away when one's friends are
    gone.
To live away from those whom one loves
Is not living at all.

Still another poem was recited:

They are gone and lost to my eyes; the body is burnt.
The shade of the shadow of the friend is gone.
If I am seen alive, parted from them so,
How can I dare to look into those eyes?

Woe to me if I am told, I am living,
So what does it matter if I am left behind?

Muhammad ibn al-Hasan al-Khalidi al-Baghdadi reports
that Ibn Khalawayh said that someone asked Ibn Jarir, "Do
you remember your father saying that if he knew that his next
meeting with his friends would not be before the Day of Last
Judgment, he would do something that he had not done
previously?" He then asked Ibn Jarir what that action would
have been. Ibn Jarir replied that his father would have taken
his eyes out to avoid seeing the parting of his friends.

(10)   Muhammad ibn Tahir al-Waziri recited this poem:

Before I heard someone say, "The ships are here,"
    I did not know the pangs of pain.
He is about to take leave; his tears are shaking him
    like a branch in the wind.
Finally waning, he left, and his last words were
    "Oh, I wish you had never been."

(11)   Help continuously and do good deeds without interrup-
tion. Hafiz 'Ali ibn 'Umar relates that al-Mahdi the Caliph
said, "There is no one who comes to me for help who has not
seen both my hands stretched out to him. Nothing pleases me
more than someone asking me for gifts for Allah's sake. If
only once one did not give what was asked for, all one had
given would be worth nothing."

(12)   Abu 'Abdullah Muhammad ibn al-'Abbas al-'Usmi relates
this advice of Ibrahim ibn Shaklah: "Once you have become
brothers with someone on this path, do not complain
anymore of his actions, whether they are right or wrong, good
or bad, whether your brother is selfish or a spendthrift who

94

throws everything away. When he is grabbing, be thankful.
When he is a spendthrift and wastes things, be patient.
Whether he is good or bad, give him his due. The right word
at the right time helps love to endure." It is also said that, at
times, "to openly reprimand is better than keeping a
grudge."

(13)   Whether a friend is with you or away from you, continue
loving him. 'Umar ibn Ahmad recites a poem of Yazid al-
Muhallabi:

> If you part from us, may God lead you
>   to beautiful places.
> When you come to us, you are always welcome.
> When you go, do not fear that we will ever forget you.
> When you come, do not feel that we will ever have
>   enough of you.

(14)   Do not lend your ears to slander against your friends.
Yusuf ibn Salih recites this poem:

> I do not hear the voice of these times,
> So I do not hear a word against my friends.
> I do not keep in my memory a single fault
>   of the ones I love.
> I protect my friends so that they need not protect me.

(15)   And do not let others know of your good actions. Abu
'Amr ibn Matar relates these words of Ibn Shibrimah: "When
good is told, there is no longer any good in it."

With Allah's will, the fifth part will follow.

PART FIVE

In the Name of Allah, the Compassionate and the Merciful;
I put my trust only in Him.

Trust and depend on your Lord alone, in any situation, at
home or abroad. It is the best guarantee. Abul-Qasim
'Abdullah ibn Muhammad al-Dimashqi advised a man who
was about to go on a journey: "My brother, do not take a
traveling companion, nor befriend anyone on your journey,
for Allah is sufficient as your companion. He is the one who
will help you to face difficulties. He is the one who will
respond to every good act with a reward. He is the one who
will ignore your faults and your mistakes, and He will be with
you at every step of your journey."

You should not wait for a need to be expressed before you
try to satisfy it, but from circumstances and signs you should
discover needs among your brothers and help before being
asked. Sheikh Abu Sahl Muhammad ibn Sulayman relates this
story from Ibn al-A'rabi: 'Umayyah ibn Abul-Salt went to visit
[Abu Zubayr] 'Abdullah ibn Jud'an. In 'Abdullah's household
were two knights of Futuwwah. They were nicknamed the
"Fireballs." 'Umayyah greeted Abu Zubayr and recited this
poem:

Need I tell you of my need, or is it enough
  for me to see that you are ashamed,
  because shame is a part of your character?
You know what justice is because you are the branch
  of such a great and honorable family tree.
Your ancestors are the possessors of benevolence,
  and the generous are not held back morning or
  evening from serving the needs of others.
Your land is the fertile land of giving
  upon which you built the house of benevolence.
You are the sky over this domain.
You race with the winds to help and to honor.
When a dog hides from the chill of the winter,
  you keep it warm in your palace.
When one praises you, he need only say a word
  and you know what his need is.

'Abdullah showed 'Umayyah the people in his company.
"Pick one of these, whomever you wish." 'Umayyah took
one man by the hand and brought him to the meeting place of
his tribe, the Quraysh. They told him, "O 'Umayyah, why did
you bring this old man, whose years are advanced and whose
bones are weak, when you could have chosen the two young
Fireballs? Why did you not pick one of them?" 'Umayyah felt
regret and went back to 'Abdullah. When 'Abdullah saw him
again, he said, "I understand; do not speak. Let me tell you
why you came." He repeated exactly what the tribe had told
him, and, pointing to one of the youths, he said, "Take this
one," and recited this poem:

  Your gift is an adornment to the man to whom you
    give it—
  But not every gift serves to adorn him.

97

That a man shows you deference does not shame him—
But sometimes to ask brings him to shame.

Hold your friend's honor higher than your own, and prefer
that you yourself be abased rather than others. Muhammad
ibn 'Abdullah reports that al-Husayn ibn 'Ali al-Qumasi
related this incident: 'Isam al-Balkhi asked to see Hatim al-
Asamm. Hatim allowed him into his presence. Later he was
asked why he had agreed to see 'Isam. Hatim answered, "In
inviting him to my presence, I saw my abasement and his
honor. In refusing to admit him, I would have seen my honor
and his abasement. I preferred his honor above mine and my
abasement over his."

In service and benevolence, you should not choose one
over another, and you should not discriminate. 'Abdullah ibn
Muhammad al-Razi says, "Humility is serving indiscrimin-
ately."

Do not give more to one and less to another. Give to
everyone, and belittle what you give, putting greater
importance on what others do. Abu 'Uthman Sa'id ibn Abu
Sa'id reports the following incident from Ja'far ibn Muhammad al-Khuldi. Abu Bakr al-Qazzaz, an Egyptian, was a good
man, and many Sufis visited him. Members of other orders
and other people often came to his house also. He treated
them all equally. Once he was asked why he was so
indiscriminate. He answered, "I am not one of those honored
men who know the inner worth of people and can tell them
apart. I fear that I might make a mistake, and I am even more
afraid to lose what I hope for."

In your appearance, use and show all the signs of good
behavior and moral character, and secretly and inwardly try to
resolve your inner states.

Abul-Husayn al-Farisi reports that Abu Muhammad al-Jurayri said, "To possessors of inner knowledge, faith has ten resources. Five of them are outward, and five of them are secret and inner. The outward values require that a person be truthful in speech, satisfied with little in wealth and property, and humble in physical appearance, and that he avoid being a burden to others or causing them sorrow, yet support the burden that they become and the sorrows that they cause without resentment. The inner values require that one prefer the presence of one's sheikh to everything, fear separation from him, hope for union with him, regret one's mistakes and faults, and have shame before one's Lord."

It is very harmful to appear in the costume of Futuwwah and assume other external signs of it before one has fulfilled its conditions and borne its heavy load. Abu 'Abdullah al-Sajazi was asked why he was not wearing the tattered and patched cloak of the path. He answered, "It would be hypocrisy to wear the clothes that identify the followers of Futuwwah before carrying on one's shoulders the weight of this path. A man can carry the attributes of Futuwwah only after he has tested whether or not he can support its weight." When he was asked about the nature of Futuwwah, he answered, "Futuwwah is knowing that others can be forgiven for their misdeeds, but that you yourself are always at fault; that everyone and everything else is complete, while you yourself are lacking. Futuwwah is showing understanding and compassion equally to what appears good and what appears bad. The highest form of Futuwwah is when nothing occupies you but Allah."

Ma'ruf al-Karkhi says, "Anyone who claims to be on this path must show these three signs: total loyalty without fear, generosity without any demand or hope for praise, and the desire to give without being asked."

(1)   Unity with one's friends, sorrow at the thought of being separated from them, and the effort to be with them always also characterize adherence to this path. In Baghdad, Abul-Hasan ibn Miqsam al-Muqri related a tale told by Muhammad ibn Yazid. An Arab had a very beautiful concubine. He admired her and was captivated by her. The man was a gambler, and he lost all his wealth. Nothing was left to him except this beautiful woman. He began to go to his friends, beg and borrow from them, and thus support his companion. When the concubine found out what he was doing, she said, "Do not do that. Sell me instead. If Allah wills, He will reunite us again." The Arab brought his concubine to 'Umar ibn 'Ubaydullah ibn Ma'mar, governor of Persia. When 'Umar saw her, he liked her very much and asked the Arab how much he wanted for her. He answered, "A hundred thousand dirhams, but she is worth much more to the one who knows her value." 'Umar bought the concubine. As the Arab was leaving with his money, the woman recited this poem:

> Let the money you took be of good use to you.
> Only my memories of you are left to me.
> When my tears surge and I tell myself,
> 'Who cares if you cry?', where should I turn but to the
>   pain in my heart?
> With whom should I converse
> And of whom should I think?

The man, casting a parting glance at the concubine, wept and recited:

100

If it were not for the tyranny of fate,
Nothing but death would have separated us.
I will put my head against the head of the pain
    of your absence, and I will speak only with it
    and think of you alone.
Farewell—we shall not see each other,
For it is left to the will of Ibn Ma'mar.

Ibn Ma'mar spoke: "If it is left to me, let it be! Take your companion and the money too." The man left in great joy with his concubine and the money, and 'Umar said, "Allah knows that I could not have bought a greater reward for my hundred thousand dirhams than to lawfully unite two lovers and save them from the terrible pain of separation."

(2)   You must give without being asked. Anything given after being asked for is merely reparation for the embarrassment suffered by the asker. The generous should not cause embarrassment to others. Abu 'Abdullah ibn Battah tells of the advice that 'Ubaydullah ibn 'Abbas gave to his brother's son. "The best of gifts is the one given without being asked, because if you are asked, what you give is only payment for the supplicant's embarrassment." 'Ubaydullah recited:

The one in embarrassment asked but received nothing,
For when he weighed what he had received,
His pain was heavier than what had been given to him.

Then he recited:

Whether you are miserly or generous,
The water pouring from your hands will not wash
The embarrassment from my face.

101

(3)   The best behavior is to see a gift of Allah in everything you receive. 'Ali ibn Muhammad al-Qazwini reports that Abu Yazid said: "If you have a friend whose relationship with you is at its worst, the relationship will certainly improve if you act according to the code of behavior. If something is given to you, be thankful to Allah, because He alone turns the hearts of others in your favor. If you suffer calamity, take refuge in repentance and patience, because your being will gather strength only with patience."

(4)   When you give, give to the ones who will know how to use what you have given. Abu 'Abdullah ibn Battah al-'Ukbari related in 'Ukbar this saying of al-Hurqah bint al-Nu'man ibn al-Mundhir to Sa'd ibn Abu Waqqas: "May Allah protect you from any harm caused by a good man, and may He prevent you from begging for your sustenance from anyone but Him. May Allah not be displeased and take His gifts away from a generous person because of you, nor make you a cause of returning a gift to the one through whose hands He gave."

(5)   Among your brethren, freely distribute what is yours. Qadi al-Mu'afa ibn Zakariyya al-Jurayri recited the following poem from the grandfather of Yahya ibn Abu Hafsah:

I was asked why I have less and less
    while everybody has more and more.
I said, "God gives me more and more generosity
    and to others, more and more wealth.

(6)   Avoid becoming the enemy of believers because of some malice they may bear. Muhammad ibn 'Abdul-Wahid al-Razi relates this advice of Salih ibn Hamzah: "Avoid being enemies of believers. The error of an otherwise good person or the enmity of the ignorant will not destroy you. Victory lies in

being defeated by good; true defeat lies in being defeated by evil. Stay away from evil so that evil will stay away from you."

Close your ears to evil words and restrain your tongue so that you will not speak them. Muhammad ibn 'Umar ibn al-Marzuban recites:

> Shut your ears to evil talk
> Just as you stop your mouth from speaking evil.
> Wake up: you become a partner in evil
> If you open your ears to evil talk.
> Many in this path lost their way with ambition,
> And death found them before they found their goal.

Just as you distribute your property freely, so should you give away your rank and position. Muhammad ibn 'Umar ibn al-Marzuban recited:

> I shall give you my life;
> Keep me in your mind and help me not to want.
> As what I am grows with what you have,
> Let my rank and honor grow with your own.

(7)   Abandon bad habits and attain good ones to form a good character within yourself. Abu 'Abdullah ibn Battah recited this poem of Ibn Masruq:

> One with a bad character has a worthless life;
> His vision narrows, as do his paths.
> No one can bear him;
> While a man of good moral is praised by all.

(8)   To protect your neighbor's rights is a good deed. It is related that the Messenger of Allah (s.a.w.s.) said: "Gabriel told me that I owe so much to my neighbor that one would think he was destined to become my heir." Abu 'Abdullah ibn Battah reports that al-Hasan al-Basri said, "The correct neighborly behavior is not to be a weight upon your neighbor, but to tolerate it when he torments you."

(9)   One is especially expected to accept, endure, and respond to the needs and wants of others. 'Abdul-Wahid ibn Ahmad al-Hashimi recites the following poem of Ibn Durayd:

> Do not be bothered by the people who want something
>   from you.
> Happy is the one from whom people want.
> Do not send away empty-handed the one who asks from
>   you,
> For lasting honor belongs to him who is the source
>   of hope.

(10)   Do not respond to harm with harm. This is the way to smooth the path of brotherhood. 'Abdullah ibn Muhammad ibn 'Abdul-Rahman reports the following saying of 'Abdullah al-Juhani: "In mutual help, the brotherhood is rejuvenated, and hostilities and revenge disappear."

(11)   Al-Husayn ibn Ahmad heard a simple Bedouin give this definition of Futuwwah: "One on the path gives food, shows a pleasant disposition, is honorable and modest, and never causes pain to anyone."

Show continuous generosity to the needy. Muhammad ibn Tahir al-Waziri recited these lines:

104

One on the path gives up all that he possesses
But never gives up his generosity.
He gives without being asked,
For he does not wish others to suffer the pain
   of asking.

On pardoning those who have caused you harm, Ja'far ibn
Ahmad ibn Abu Za'id al-Misri mentions this poem by Mansur,
recited by his father:

My sin is great, but You are greater than my sin.
Give Your pardon first, then cleanse me of my sin.
In my need I lost all grace.
You are the Grace, the Giver.

Ja'far also recited this poem of Mansur the Jurist:

If you see my faults, forgive them.
Is this not an obligation of brotherhood?
If you cause harm as I do,
Where is your kindness and your generosity?

Retire to seclusion when times are bad. Abu Bakr ibn Abu
Ja'far al-Muzakki recites the following lines from a poem by
al-Hakim 'Abdul-Hamid ibn 'Abdul-Rahman:

Hand in hand with my loneliness I retire to my corner;
In total solitude, happiness thrives.
The times have educated me. How much better it would
   have been
Had I gone to far places where I could not find anyone,
   nor anyone me!

Then as long as I lived, I would never have had to say
The soldiers are marching and the princes are mounting
   their horses.

(12)   Know and obey the principles of kindness as related by
Muhammad ibn al-'Abbas and set forth by Zafir ibn
Sulayman: "A man who is truly kind protects his faith, visits
his relatives, improves his property, is generous to his
brethren, and is discreet."

When a friend is in a desparate situation, aid him and
protect his rights. Sheikh Abu Sahl Muhammad ibn Sulayman
relates that Abu Salim showed devoted attachment to his
relative 'Ali ibn 'Isa, and served him day and night. But when
Abu Salim was appointed to the high position of vizier in the
government, he was not able to give 'Ali the same attention as
before. 'Ali wrote him a letter, saying:

My whole life I wished you would become a vizier.
Now that my hopes are granted, people who could not
speak when I was with you come before me. I really
wish to die because this life which I resent now is more
than death.

(13)   'Ali ibn Hamdan recites the following poem of Ibrahim ibn
al-'Abbas:

You were a good brother to me
   during the fraternity of good times,
But as times changed,
   you became my adversary.
I used to save you from ill and evil;
Now I have to beg you to be relieved.

I used to complain of the times to you;
You see now I miss those times,
    which I prefer to you as you are now.

14)   Help and give to all without discrimination. Abul-Hasan
ibn Muqsim declared in Baghdad that al-Mada'ini told that the
last advice of Yahya ibn Khalid al-Barmaki to his son was to
be generous to mankind always, because giving to others is
giving to oneself.

Respect the rights of people's homes, for the sake of the
respect you must show to those who abide there. Abul-Fadl
al-Sukri told a story from Abu 'Amr Muhammad ibn Isma'il:
"I heard that a woman entered the castle of Sufyan ibn 'Asim.
She rolled in the dust of the gardens and wrote on the walls,
'For one who loves, to see the domains of the beloved an
abandoned desert is sufficient for sorrow. Dwelling in them
from morning till night he does not see them, nor notice that
an age has settled upon them. The lover given over to
patience finds that love increases with the pain of patience.'
And she signed her name on the wall: Aminah, daughter of
'Abdul-'Aziz, wife of Sufyan ibn 'Asim."

If you love someone, love unconditionally, and beware of
being disloyal. Abul-Mufaddal al-Shaybani reports this saying
from Sufyan ibn 'Uyaynah: "The path of Futuwwah is called a
brotherhood because it is composed of those who avoid
disloyalty at all costs; and its members are called faithful
because they are loyal to their love for each other."

When one knows what the true love of a friend is, one can
never speak ill of him. Muhammad ibn Ahmad ibn Tawbah al-
Maruzi says: "If you know that someone truly loves you, all of
his faults are already forgiven; if you know someone as an

107

enemy, all of his good deeds cannot be recognized. May Allah guide you with His divine care. Know that the essence of Futuwwah is to care for your faith, to abide with the prescriptions of the Prophet (s.a.w.s.), and to act according to Allah's orders to His own Prophet (s.a.w.s.): 'Take to forgiveness, enjoin good, and turn away from the ignorant' [Koran 7:199] and 'Allah orders justice, the doing of good, and giving to relatives, and forbids indecency, evil, and rebellion, and He gives you advice so that you will be mindful' '' [Koran 16:90].

Know that Futuwwah means following the honored words of the Prophet (s.a.w.s.) on the day he entered Mecca: "O my people, give salutations, wish the blessings of Allah upon each other, feed each other, visit your relatives, pray in the quiet of the night when all else is asleep, and enter salvation and Paradise.''

And know that Futuwwah is gained by avoiding what our Master forbids: "Do not stay away from your family, do not turn your backs on each other, O good servants of Allah, be brothers to each other as Allah orders you to do.''

Be honest, loyal, and dependable; be generous; keep a beautiful character; be satisfied with little; do not make fun of your friends, and live with them in harmony; do not listen to slander; wish to do good; be a good neighbor; speak well and be loyal to your word; treat your household and those who are dependent upon you well; treat those who serve you well; educate the young and teach them good behavior; respect your elders and superiors; refrain from holding grudges and seeking vengeance; do not cheat or manipulate people, or criticize or talk against them.

Love for Allah's sake and hate for Allah's sake. Be friends

for Allah's sake and be enemies for Allah's sake. Distribute freely from your property and help others from the rank that has been bestowed upon you. Do not expect appreciation or praise; give when you are asked to show your wealth and your position; serve your guests with your own hands, and serve and give lovingly, not grudgingly. Feed your friends from your own food and show them respect; meet the needs of your brethren with your property and your very life; respond to others' faults with kindness; visit those who do not visit you; be humble and avoid arrogance; avoid self-love and do not think highly of your state. Do good consistently to your mother and father; visit your kin; do not see the faults of others, keep secret their wrongdoings, and advise them only when no one can hear; pray for the sinners and pardon their wrongdoings. Feel the evil and the terror of your ego, and the shame of going along with it. Show consideration to people and compassion, kindness, and good to the faithful and the Muslims. Pity the poor and be compassionate toward the rich; be modest before men of knowledge; discern the truth in what you hear and accept it. Save your tongue from lies and slander, save your ears from error, and save your eyes from looking at the unlawful. Be sincere and pure in your actions, be straight in your states. See what is good and beautiful in the Creation; escape from the evil and befriend the good. Turn away from the wordly and face Allah. Leave your wants; throw away the desire to be praised for your worldly achievement. Be honored by the company of the poor. Avoid respecting the rich for their riches; the real wealth is to be with one's Lord. Be thankful for what is given to you. Tell the truth without fearing anybody. Offer thanks for things in which you find joy, and be patient with the difficulties that you have to tolerate. Flee from the curse of disloyalty and keep others' secrets. When you are with company, sit at a place below that which is due to your rank. Give up your rights, while fully upholding the rights of others. Educate your ego. Abide by Allah's prohibitions when you are by yourself. Consult your friends in every matter. Trust in Allah when you are in need. Do not be ambitious. Show respect to the devout, show kindness to the sinful. Do not cause discomfort to anyone; let your outer self be the same as your inner self. Be friends with the friend of your friend and enemies with the enemy of your friend. No matter how far away your friend is, be with him.

These are some of the signs of the ones who follow the path of Futuwwah. May Allah bestow upon us the good nature that He likes in His servants. May He sustain us with the character of the path. May He forgive us for our casualness with our time and with our states. May He bring us to the possibility of action that meets with His approval, and may He bring us to His proximity. He is near us; He is the One Who accepts prayers.

All praise is due to the Lord of the Worlds. May Allah send His continuous blessings and salutations to our Master, the Master of all Prophets, Muhammad (s.a.w.s.), and his pure progeny and his companions.

ISNAD

PART ONE

1. Ahmad b. Muhammad b. Raja' al-Abzari—Ahmad b. 'Umayr b. Jawsa'—Abu 'Umayr 'Isa b. Muhammad—Muhammad b. Yusuf—Sufyan—Thawr b. Yazid—Rashid—Mu'awiyah.
2. 'Abdullah b. Muhammad b. 'Ali b. Ziyad—Muhammad b. Ishaq al-Thaqafi—Sa'id b. Yahya—his father—Yazid b. Kaysan—Abu Hazim—Abu Hurayrah.
3. Muhammad b. 'Abdullah b. Muhammad b. Sabih—'Abdullah b. Shiruyah—Ishaq al-Hanzali—Jarir—Abu Hazim—Abu Hurayrah.
4. Abul-Qasim Ibrahim b. Muhammad al-Nasrabadhi—Muhammad b. Rabi'—Sulayman al-Jizi in Egypt—his father—Talq b. al-Samh—Yahya b. Ayyub—Hamid—Anas.
5. Muhammad b. Muhammad b. Ya'qub al-Hafiz—'Abdullah b. Ayyub al-'Asqalani—Hashim b. Muhammad al-Ansari—'Amr b. Bakr—'Abbad—Ayyub b. Musa and Isma'il b. 'Umayyah—Nafi'—Ibn 'Umar.
6. Muhammad b. Muhammad b. Ya'qub al-Hajjaji—'Abdullah b. Salih al-Mada'ini in al-Misaysah—Abul-Darda' Hashim b. Ya'la—'Amr b. Bakr—Abu Jurayj—'Ata' b. Jabir.

7. Abul-Husayn b. Sabih—Muhammad b. al-Musayyab al-Arghiyani—'Abdul-Rahman b. al-Harith—Baqiyyah b. al-Walid—al-Awza'i—al-Zuhri—'A'ishah.

8. Muhammad b. Muhammad al-Faqih al-Maruzi—Muhammad b. 'Umayr al-Razi—Ishaq b. Ibrahim b. Yunus—Husayn b. Marzuq al-Nawfali—'Abdullah b. Ibrahim al-Safari—'Abdullah b. Abu Bakr, nephew of Muhammad b. al-Munkadar—Safwan b. Sulaym—'Ata'—'A'ishah.

9. Ibrahim b. Muhammad b. Yahya—Habshun b. Musa al-Khallal—Muhammad b. Hassan—Qabisah—Sufyan—Abdul-Malik b. Abu Bashir—'Abdullah b. Abul-Musawir.

10. Ibrahim b. Ahmad al-Abzari—al-Husayn b. 'Ali b. Zakariyya al-Basri—'Uthman b. 'Amr al-Dabbagh—Ibn 'Ulathah—al-Awza'i—Yahya b. Abu Kathir—Ja'far—Abu Hurayrah.

11. Isma'il b. Ahmad al-Khallali*—Abu Badr Ahmad b. Khalid b. 'Abdul-Malik—Makhlid b. Yazid—Abu Dawud al-Nakh'i—Abul-Juwayriyyah—Ibn al-'Abbas.

12. Isma'il b. Ahmad al-Khallali—Muhammad b. al-Husayn b. Qutaybah—Ishaq b. Ibrahim b. Suwayd—Isma'il b. Uways—his father—Muhammad b. al-Mundakar—Abu Sa'id al-Khudri.

13. Isma'il b. Ahmad al-Khallali—Muhammad b. al-Husayn b. Qutaybah—Hamid b. Yahya—Sufyan—'Ata' b. al-Sa'ib—his father—'Ali.

---

*In *Mu'jam al-buldan* by Yaqut, the author gives the full name as Isma'il b. Ahmad b. Muhammad al-Khallali. —Trans.

14. Muhammad b. 'Abdullah b. Zakariyya—Ahmad b. al-Husayn al-Hafiz and Makki b. 'Abdan—Muhammad b. Yahya al-Duhli—'Abdul-Razzaq—Ma'mar—al-Zuhri—Ibn al-Musayyab.

15. Muhammad b. 'Abdullah b. Muhammad b. Quraysh—al-Husayn b. Sufyan—Muhammad b. Rumh—Ibn Luhay'ah—Yazid b. Abu Habib—Abul-Khayr—'Uqbah b. 'Amir.

16. Isma'il b. 'Abdullah Mikali and 'Ali b. Sa'd al-'Askari—Ja'far b. al-Fadl al-Rasibi—Muhammad b. Yusuf al-Firyabi—Abul-Aswad Mujahid b. Farqad al-Atrabulusi—Wathilah b. al-Khattab al-Qurashi.

17. Abu 'Amr Muhammad b. Ja'far, Ibn Matar, and Muhammad b. Ibrahim b. 'Abdah—Yahya b. Yahya—'Abdul-Rahman b. Abul-Zinad—his father—'Urwah.

18. Abu Bakr al-Diwanji—al-Husayn b. Sufyan—'Uthman b. Sa'id—Muhammad b. 'Imran b. Abu Bakr—Sulayman b. Raja'—Salih al-Mari'—al-Hasan—Abu Sa'id al-Khudri.

19. Abu 'Amr and Muhammad b. Ahmad b. Hamdan—'Imran b. Musa al-Sakhtiyani—Shayban b. Abu Shaybah—Abul-Asshab—Abu Nadrah—Abu Sa'id al-Khudri.

20. Muhammad b. 'Abdullah b. Sabih—'Abdullah b. Shiruyah—Ishaq al-Hanzali—al-Nadr b. Shumayl—Shu'bah—Ya'la b. 'Ata'—al-Walid b. 'Abdul-Rahman—Abu Idris al-Khawlani.

21. 'Abdullah b. Muhammad b. 'Ali b. Ziyad—Muhammad b. Ishaq b. Khuzaymah—Abu Shu'ayb—Muhammad b. Muslim—Muhammad b. 'Abdullah b. Aws—Sulayman b. Hurmuz—'Abdullah b. 'Amr.

22. 'Abdullah b. Muhammad al-Simidi—'Abdullah b.

Muhammad b. 'Abdul-Rahman—Ishaq b. Ibrahim—
Yahya b. Yahya—Ibn Luhay'ah—al-Harith b. Zayd—Ibn
Hujayrah—'Abdullah b. 'Amr.

23. 'Abdullah b. Ahmad b. Ja'far al-Shaybani—Ahmad b.
Muhammad b. 'Ali al-Bashani—Ahmad b. 'Abdullah al-
Juwayri—Salm b. Salim—'Abbad b. Kathir—Malik b.
Dinar—al-Hasan.

24. Muhammad b. al-Fadl b. Muhammad b. Ishaq al-
Thaqafi—Ishaq al-Hanzali—Hazim—Abu Hurayrah.

25. Muhammad b. Ya'qub al-Asamm—al-'Abbas b.
Muhammad al-Duri—Yahya b. Mu'in—'Abdul-Rahman
Bayya' al-Harawi—Ja'far b. Muhammad—his father.

26. 'Abdullah b. Muhammad b. 'Ali—Abul-'Abbas al-
Thaqafi—al-Husayn b. 'Isa—Ibn al-Mubarak—Sufyan—
Abu Ishaq al-Hamdani—'Amr b. Shurahbil—'A'ishah.

27. Muhammad b. 'Abdullah b. Muhammad b. Quraysh—
Musaddid b. Qatn—Dawud b. Rashid—Baqiyyah—
Muhammad b. 'Abdul-Rahman—'Ubaydullah—Nafi'—
Ibn 'Umar.

28. 'Abdul-'Aziz b. Ja'far b. Muhammad al-Khirqani in
Baghdad—Muhammad b. Harun b. Buwayh—'Isa b.
Mihran—al-Hasan b. al-Husayn—al-Husayn b. Zayd.

29. Abul-Faraj al-Sa'igh—al-Husayn b. Sahl—Ahmad b.
'Umar al-Razi—'Ali b. Salih—'Imran b. Musa al-
Dabili—his father.

30. Abu Bakr al-Razi—Abu 'Uthman al-Adami—Ibrahim al-
Khawwas.

31. Abu Bakr al-Razi—Khayr al-Nassaj—Abu Hamzah.

32. Muhammad b. Shadhan—'Ali b. Musa al-Tahirti.

33. Abu Bakr al-Razi—Sa'id al-Sufi—Ibn Yazdanyar.

34. Abul-Tayyib al-Shirazi—Abu Bakr al-Tamastani.

35. Ahmad b. Muhammad b. Zakariyya—'Ali b. Ibrahim—
    Ibrahim b. Shayban—Sahl b. 'Abdullah.
36. Abul-'Abbas Ahmad b. Muhammad al-Nisawi—Ahman
    b. 'Ata'—'Ali b. Ja'far—Ahmad b. Ibrahim al-Suri—al-
    Musayyab b. Wadih.
37. 'Abdul-Wahid b. Bakr—'Abdullah b. Ahmad al-
    Naqid—Ahmad b. al-Salt—Bishr al-Harith.
38. Muhammad b. 'Abdullah—Sa'id b. 'Uthman al-'Abbas.
39. Muhammad b. 'Abdullah al-'Aziz—Yusuf b. al-Husayn—
    Dhu Nun.
40. Abul-Husayn al-Farisi—Ahmad b. 'Ali—al-Kattani.

PART TWO

1. Abul-Husayn al-Farisi—Ibn 'Alawiyyah.
2. Abul-Husayn al-Farisi.
3. Muhammad b. Ahmad b. Ibrahim al-Nisawi—Ja'far b.
   Muhammad b. Nasir.
4. Abul-Husayn al-Farisi—al-Husayn b. Hamdan—his
   father.
5. Abul-Husayn al-Farisi—Ibn 'Isam.
6. Abul-Husayn al-Farisi—Muhammad b. al-Hasan—'Ali b.
   'Abdul-Hamid al-Ghudari.
7. Muhammad b. Tahir al-Waziri—al-Hasan b. Muhammad
   b. Ishaq—Ibn 'Uthman.
8. 'Abdullah b. Muhammad b. Isfandiyar—al-Husayn b.
   'Alawiyyah.
9. Abul-Husayn 'Ali b. Muhammad al-Qazwini al-Sufi.
10. Abul-Husayn al-Qazwini—Ja'far al-Khuldi—Ibn
    Masruq—Muhammad b. Bashir.

11. Abul-'Abbas Muhammad b. al-Hasan al-Baghdadi— Muhammad b. 'Abdullah al-Farghani.

12. Muhammad b. al-Hasan al-Khashshab—Ahmad b. Muhammad b. Salih—Muhammad b. 'Abdun.

13. Abul-'Abbas b. al-Khashshab—Muhammad b. 'Abdullah al-Farghani.

14. Muhammad b. al-Hasan b. Khuld—Abu Ja'far al-Farghani.

15. Muhammad b. al-Hasan al-Baghdadi—Ahmad b. Muhammad b. Salih—Muhammad b. 'Abdun—'Abdus b. al-Qasim.

16. Abul-Faraj al-Warthani—Mansur b. Ahmad al-Harawi— Abul-Husayn Muhammad b. 'Ali al-Khwarizmi.

17. 'Abdul-Wahid b. Bakr—Abu Bakr Muhammad b. 'Abdullah al-Dinawari—'Abdullah b. Muhammad al-Harith al-Sufi.

18. Abul-Faraj al-Warthani—Ibrahim b. Ahmad al-Saji— Muhammad b. al-Husayn al-Khasib—al-'Abbas b. 'Abdul-Azim.

19. 'Abdul-Wahid b. Bakr—Muhammad b. 'Abdul-Aziz.

20. 'Abdul-Wahid b. Bakr—Muhammad b. Harun al-Ansari—'Isa b. al-Ra'is al-Anmati al-Maruzi.

21. Ahmad b. Muhammad b. Ya'qub—Ahmad b. Muhammad b. 'Ali—'Ali al-Razi.

22. Abu Ahmad al-Hafiz—Ahmad b. 'Ubaydullah al-Razi in Antioch—Ja'far b. 'Abdul-Wahid—Abu 'Ubaydah Mu'ammar b. al-Muthanna and Muhammad b. al-Harith al-Hilali—Malik b. 'Atiyyah—his father—Abu Rifa'ah al-Fahmi—Abu Bakr al-Siddiq.

23. Ahmad b. Muhammad b. Ya'qub—Ahmad b. 'Ata'— 'Umar b. Mukhallad al-Sufi—Ibn Abul-Ward.

24. Abu Bakr al-Jurjani—Abu Bakr b. Muhammad b. Ja'far— Abu Bakr b. 'Abdul-Jalil.

25. Abu Bakr al-Razi—Abu Muhammad al-Jurayri.
26. Muhammad b. 'Abdullah b. Shadhan—Ja'far b. Muhammad.
27. Abu Sa'id al-Razi—Abul-Hasan al-Mihlabi al-Baghdadi.
28. 'Abdullah b. Muhammad b. Isfandiyar in Damghan— al-Hasan b. 'Alawiyyah.
29. Abul-Hasan b. Qatadah al-Balkhi—al-Qannad.
30. Sa'id b. Muhammad al-Shashi—al-Haytham b. Kulayb.
31. Al-Husayn b. Yahya—Ja'far b. Muhammad—'Ali b. Musa al-Tahrani.
32. 'Abdullah b. 'Ali al-Sarraj—'Abdul-Karim b. Ahmad b. 'Abdullah—al-Husayn b. Abu Sahl al-Simsar—Hasan al-Khayyat.
33. Abul-Fadl Nadr b. Abu Nasr al-'Attar—Ahmad b. al-Husayn al-Harrani in Kufa—Hilal b. al-'Ala'.
34. Abul-Fadl Nadr b. Abu Nasr al-'Attar—'Umar b. al-Ushnani al-Qadi—Ibn Abul-Dunya—Ishaq b. Isma'il.
35. Nasr b. Muhammad b. Ahmad al-Sufi—Sulayman b. Abu Salamah al-Faqih—al-Qasim b. 'Abdul-Rahman.
36. Nasr b. Muhammad b. Ahmad b. Ya'qub—Ja'far b. Muhammad b. Nasr.
37. Mansur b. 'Abdullah al-Khawass—al-Taflisi.

PART THREE

1. Mansur b. 'Abdullah—Abu Ja'far al-Anmati—Ibrahim b. Bashhar—Ibn 'Uyaynah.
2. Mansur b. 'Abdullah—al-Qasim b. 'Ubaydullah in Basra—al Husayn b. Nasr—'Ali b. Musa al-Rida.
3. 'Abdullah b. Muhammad b. Isfandiyar in Damghan—al-Husayn b. 'Alawiyyah.

4. Abu Bakr b. Ahyad.
5. Abul-Husayn b. Muqsim—Ja'far al-Khuldi.
6. Abul-'Abbas al-Baghdadi—Muhammad ibn 'Abdullah al-Farghani.
7. Muhammad b. al-Hasan—Ahmad b. Muhammad b. Salih—Muhammad b. 'Abdun.
8. Muhammad b. al-Hasan al-Khalidi—Ahmad b. Muhammad b. Salih—Muhammad b. 'Abdun—'Abdus b. al-Qasim.
9. Abul-'Abbas al-Khashshab—Abul-Fadl al-Nisaburi—Sa'id b. 'Uthman.
10. Abul-'Abbas Muhammad b. al-Hasan b. Muhammad b. Khalidi—Ahmad b. Muhammad b. Salih—Ibn Yazdanyar.
11. Abul-'Abbas al-Makhrami—Muhammad b. 'Abdullah al-Farghani.
12. 'Abdullah b. Muhammad b. Isfandiyar—al-Hasan b. 'Alawiyyah.
13. 'Ubaydullah b. 'Uthman b. Yahya—Ja'far b. Muhammad b. Nusayr b. Masruq.
14. 'Abdullah b. Muhammad al-Damghani—al-Hasan b. 'Alawiyyah.
15. 'Abdullah b. 'Uthman b. Yahya—Ja'far al-Khuldi—Muhammad b. al-Fadl—Ahmad b. Shahqawiyyah.
16. 'Ubaydullah b. Yahya—Ja'far—Muhammad b. al-Fadl—Ahmad b. Khalaf—Ahmad b. Shahawiyyah.
17. Muhammad b. 'Abdullah b. Shadhan—Abu Bakr al-Harbi.
18. Abu Bakr al-Razi—'Umar al-Bistami—his father.
19. Abu Bakr al-Razi—Muhammad b. 'Abdullah—Ja'far b. Nusayr.
20. 'Abdullah b. Muhammad b. Isfandiyar al-Damghani—al-Hasan b. 'Alawiyyah.

21. 'Abdullah b. Muhammad b. Isfandiyar al-Damghani—al-Hasan b. —Alawiyyah.

PART FOUR

1. Abu Sahl Muhammad b. Sulayman—Ibn al-Anbari.
2. Muhammad b. 'Abdullah al-Razi—Ja'far b. Muhammad al-Khawwas.
3. Abu Bakr al-Mufid—al-Husayn b. Isma'il al-Rab'i—al-Fihri.
4. Abul-Husayn al-Farisi—Ja'far al-Khuldi.
5. Al-Sulami's grandfather.
6. Abul-Husayn al-Farisi—Abu 'Ali al-Ansari.
7. 'Ali b. al-Hasan b. Ja'far al-Rida al-Hafiz in Baghdad—Ahmad b. al-Hasan Dubays al-Khayyat—Sulayman b. al-Fadl al-Balkhi.
8. Al-Rashid—al-Mahdi—al-Mansur—his father—'Ukrumah—Ibn 'Abbas—Jarir b. 'Abdullah.
9. 'Ali b. 'Umar al-Hafiz in Baghdad—Yazdan al-Katib.
10. Muhammad b. Tahir al-Waziri—Sa'id b. 'Abdullah al-Baghdadi.
11. 'Ali b. 'Umar al-Hafiz—al-Hasan b. Isma'il al-Qadi—'Abdullah b. Abu Sa'id—Harun b. Maymun—Abu Khuzaymah Ilban 'Isa.
12. Abu 'Abdullah Muhammad b. al-'Abbas al-'Usmi—Muhammad b. Abu 'Ali al-Khalladi—Muhammad b. al-Hasan al-Ramli—'Ali b. Muhammad al-Marhani—Muhammad b. Ibrahim b. Ishaq al-'Abbasi—'Abdullah b. al-Hajjaj, who was a client (mawla) of al-Mahdi.
13. 'Umar b. Ahmad b. 'Uthman—Ibn al-Anbari.
14. Yusuf b. Salih—Ibn al-Anbari.

15. Abu 'Amr b. Matar—Ja'far b. Ahmad b. Nasr al-Hafiz—
'Ali b. Khashram—Muhammad b. al-Fudayl.

PART FIVE

1. Abul-Hasan b. Miqsam al-Muqri'—Abul-'Abbas al-Katib
al-'Aquli.
2. Abu 'Abdullah b. Battah—al-Hassan b. Muhammad b. al-
Hasan in Kufa—Muhammad b. al-Marzuban—'Abdul-
Rahman b. Muhammad—Muhammad b. Salih al-
Qurashi—Abul-Yaqzan—Abu 'Amr al-Madini—al-
Husayn b.'Abdullah b. 'Ubaydullah b. 'Abbas.
3. 'Ali b. Muhammad al-Qazwini—Abu Tayyib al-'Akki—
Ibn al-Anbari—a student of Abu Yazid's.
4. Abu 'Abdullah b. Battah al-'Ukbari in 'Ukbar—
Muhammad b. Ahmad b. Thabit—Ahmad b. 'Amr b.
Hamdun—al- Hasan b. 'Arafah—Hisham b. Muhammad
—his father.
5. Al-Mu'afa b. Zakariyya al-Qadi al-Jurayri in Baghdad—
al-Hasan b. al-Qasim—Abu Ja'far—Sulayman b. Yahya
b. Abu Hafsah.
6. Muhammad b. 'Abdul-Wahid al-Razi—Muhammad b.
'Ali b. 'Abduk—Zakariyya b. Yahya al-Nisaburi—
Ibrahim b. al-Junayd.
7. Abu 'Abdullah b. Battah—Abul-Husayn al-Harbi.
8. Abu 'Abdullah b. Battah—Isma'il b. 'Abdullah b. al-
'Abbas al-Warraq—Ja'far al-Sa'igh—Ahmad b. al-
Tayyib—Abul-Fath al-Raqqi.
9. 'Abdul-Wahid b. Ahmad al-Hashimi—'Abdullah b.
Yahya al-'Uthmani.

10. 'Abdullah b. Muhammad b. 'Abdul-Rahman—Ishaq b. Ibrahim b. Abu Hassan—Ahmad b. Abul-Hawari—Abul-Mughayyis.
11. Al-Husayn b. Ahmad b. Musa—Ibn al-Anbari—Ahmad b. Yahya—Ibn al-A'rabi.
12. Muhammad b. Yahya al-'Usmi—Muhammad b. Abu 'Ali b. al-'Abbas—Ahmad b. 'Ali al-Kindi—al-Hasan b. Salim—Yahya b. Salim.
13. 'Ali b. Hamdan—Ibn al-Anbari.
14. Abul-Hasan b. Muqsim in Baghdad—Muhammad b. Ishaq al-Marwazi—his father.

BOOKS OF RELATED INTEREST

Muhammad
His Life Based on the Earliest Sources
by Martin Lings

The Forbidden Rumi
The Suppressed Poems of Rumi on Love,
Heresy, and Intoxication
Translations and Commentary by
Nevit O. Ergin and Will Johnson

The Rubais of Rumi
Insane with Love
Translations and Commentary by
Nevit O. Ergin and Will Johnson

The Spiritual Practices of Rumi
Radical Techniques for Beholding the Divine
by Will Johnson

Rumi's Four Essential Practices
Ecstatic Body, Awakened Soul
by Will Johnson

Islamic Patterns
An Analytical and Cosmological Approach
by Keith Critchlow

Journey to the Lord of Power
A Sufi Manual on Retreat
by Ibn Arabi, with commentary by Abd al-Kerim al-Jili
Translated from the Arabic by Rabia Terry Harris

The Book of Sufi Healing
by Shaykh Hakim Moinuddin Chishti

Inner Traditions • Bear & Company
P.O. Box 388
Rochester, VT 05767
1-800-246-8648
www.InnerTraditions.com

Or contact your local bookseller